How to Make Your *Writing* Reader-Friendly

How to Make Your
Writing
Reader-Friendly

Richard Dowis

BETTERWAY PUBLICATIONS, INC.
WHITE HALL, VIRGINIA

Published by Betterway Publications, Inc.
P.O. Box 219
Crozet, VA 22932
(804) 823-5661

Cover design by Susan Riley
Typography by East Coast Typography

Library of Congress Cataloging-in-Publication Data

Dowis, Richard
    How to make your writing reader-friendly : a self-help
manual for people who want to write better / Richard Dowis.
        p. cm.
    Includes bibliographical references.
    ISBN 1-55870-148-6 : $7.95
    1. Authorship–Handbooks, manuals, etc.   2. Business
writing—Handbooks, manuals, etc.   I. Title.
    PN147.D69   1990   89-29931
    808'.042–dc20   CIP

Printed in the United States of America
0 9 8 7 6 5 4 3 2 1

*This book is dedicated to my best friend,
my staunchest supporter, my severest critic,
and my only lover —
my wife, Ouida Woods Dowis*

ACKNOWLEDGMENTS

The decision to write this book did not come in a flash of inspiration. It began as a a vague notion and grew over time, nourished by the encouragement I received from my colleagues at Manning, Selvage & Lee, Inc. Two of these colleagues have earned my special gratitude: Lydia Griffin for her eagle eye and boundless enthusiasm, and Joe Ledlie for his tireless and thorough editing of my second draft.

I also want to acknowledge the contributions of the men and women who have participated in my business-writing seminar, "Effective Writing for Success in Business." I learned as much from them as they learned from me, which I suppose is something that could be said of most successful seminars.

Finally, my thanks to Dixie Dowis McGinty, who read the manuscript with a critic's eye and a daughter's love.

Contents

*Break any of these rules sooner than
say anything outright barbarous.*

*— George Orwell,
"Politics and the English Language"*

Introduction

In computer jargon, equipment that does what it is supposed to do without taxing the user unduly is called "user-friendly." Writing is "reader-friendly" when it imparts its message without taxing the reader unduly. Far too little business writing can be called reader-friendly.

How To Make Your Writing Reader-Friendly is for people who want to write better. It's primarily for writers of letters, memos, reports, news releases, business plans, and other business-oriented materials, but the principles of reader-friendly writing apply to *all* types of writing.

The book grew out of a seminar on better business writing that I developed for Manning, Selvage & Lee, one of the nation's most respected public relations agencies. The premise of the book and of the seminar on which the book is based is simple: Everyone *needs* to write better, and almost everyone *can learn* to write better.

I fell in love with writing when I was in the fourth grade. My teacher liked a paragraph I had written, and she asked me to read it to the class. It was about a heroic trainman who miraculously stopped his train in the nick of time to save a puppy whose paw had become wedged between a rail and a crosstie. It was inspired — or so it seemed to me at the time.

From that day I was hooked. I did not learn until years later that the role of inspiration in writing is minimal and that writing is hard work even for the best writers. I also learned that writing is a skill that can be acquired through study and practice. Once I understood that, I began to take apart sentences and paragraphs and stories, as a mechanic might take apart an engine to understand better how it functions. This book delves into some of the mechanics of writing, for the best writing is done by people who understand not only what works in writing but also why it works.

By learning and applying diligently the fundamentals of good writing that are discussed in the book, you can improve your writing. Even if you already write well, you can improve. How much you improve and how fast you improve depend on how diligently you apply the principles and how much you practice. The book is a start. It can be a good start. It will likely be a *re*learning experience, because you almost certainly have encountered some of the principles before. It can help you gain confidence in your ability to write.

Finally, this book can give you a new appreciation of the power and grace and efficiency of a well-crafted sentence. If it does that — and only that — the time you spend with it will be time well spent.

HOW TO USE THE BOOK

How To Make Your Writing Reader-Friendly is designed to make the reader feel as if he or she is participating in a seminar on writing. The text and the examples are intended both to inform readers and to stimulate their thinking. Because much of the material is taken from my writing seminar, its instructional value is firmly established through several years of use.

The organization of the book is much like that of my seminar: presentation of instructional material, work by participants on exercises, discussion and critique of participants' work. You could sit in on a seminar and learn a lot simply by listening; but you could learn more by participating actively. This principle applies also to using this book. You can learn a lot about clear writing by reading the material. You can learn more if you follow this sequence: (a) read the material and the illustrations in each section, (b) work on the exercise related to each before going on to the next section, and (c) compare your work on each exercise with my "solution." Exercises are discussed in Appendix A.

Here are some additional suggestions for using the book:

1. If possible, enlist a friend to work with you. The mutual reinforcement will be invaluable.

2. Don't rush. Take time to read the text and the examples two or three times and to think carefully about what you have read. Do careful, thorough work on the exercises. Made certain you understand the principles in one section before you go on to the next.

3. Become conscious of good and bad writing, and try to determine what makes it bad or good. Start a collection of writing samples that illustrate the principles discussed in the book.

4. Retain your exercises so that you can compare them with future work to see whether your writing has improved.

5. Reread the book about every six months. Even the best writers fall into bad habits.

6. Practice, practice, practice. That's the only way you'll improve.

1.
What Makes Good Writing

... [W]riting comes in grades of quality in the fashion of beer and baseball games: good, better, best. ... Better ways can be mastered by writers who are serious about their writing. There is nothing arcane or mysterious about the crafting of a good sentence.
— James J. Kilpatrick, *The Writer's Art*

James Kilpatrick is right. There is nothing mysterious about writing. Why, then, are business communications so often written in such tortuous sentences? Why does so much of the stuff that crosses America's desks every day sound as if the writer intended to keep its meaning secret? Why do otherwise intelligent and resourceful men and women turn mush-brained when they face the task of putting words on paper?

The answer to these questions is multifaceted, but one part of the answer is that many people simply don't know what makes good writing. Some evidently believe that good writing cannot be simple and direct. If it is, it will not be impressive. Imagine, if you can stretch your imagination far enough, that the human-resources director of a large American company died and went to heaven and was assigned the task of rewriting the Bible to make it more appealing to business people. Instead of opening with "In the beginning, God created heaven and earth," he or she probably would write something like this: "Early on, God successfully and effectively fabricated the heaven above and the planet earth on a timely basis."

I do not mean to single out personnel managers. Engineers, accountants, sales people, lawyers, and executives are capable of producing turgid prose.

In *The Writer's Art,* Kilpatrick cites a sentence from the back of a Crest toothpaste tube: "FOR BEST RESULTS, SQUEEZE THE TUBE FROM THE BOTTOM AND FLATTEN IT AS YOU GO UP." That sentence, he says, can't be improved. I agree. The world's best writer couldn't make it better. The reason is, *it does exactly what it is supposed to do.* No more, no less. Every word in the sentence has its function; nothing should be omitted, nothing added. Kilpatrick does not suggest, nor do I, that the English language is seen in all its splendor on the back of a toothpaste tube. He does suggest that the sentence is a perfect example of functional writing: It uses simple words arranged logically to convey meaning that cannot be misunderstood.

But words alone do not create meaning. If they did, a thesaurus would be the most useful book you could own. You would need nothing more than a big vocabulary to be a good writer. We create meaning by how we use words, how we make them into sentences and arrange the sentences into paragraphs, and how we organize our material. Often, the words we choose *not* to use are more important than the ones we use.

SOME MYTHS ABOUT WRITERS AND WRITING

People have strange ideas about writers and writing. These ideas range from the notion that writing is so easy that "anyone with half a brain can do it" to the notion that only "creative" people can write, and ordinary mortals shouldn't even try. It's no wonder many people are confused about what makes good writing.

During more than thirty years as a professional writer and editor, I have seen and heard these and other misconceptions about writing and writers expressed often and in many ways. I call them "myths about writers and writing."

MYTH NUMBER ONE: *To write well, just write the way you speak.* Writing and speaking are different ways of communicating. When you talk, you use eye contact, facial expressions, and gestures. You can raise or lower your voice. You can repeat points of emphasis without being tedious.

But when you write, your options are fewer.

I recall Robert MacFarlane's testimony in the Iran-Contra hearings in the summer of 1987. It seemed lucid and well organized when I heard it on television, but it seemed fuzzy and rambling when I read it in the newspaper.

People who advise you to write the way you speak — and they include some writing teachers — probably mean that you should cultivate a relaxed, natural style so that you *seem* to write the way you speak.

Good writing often seems to duplicate the rhythms of natural speech. As an example, consider the following pair of sentences:

> This year the company experienced United States sales representative recruiting difficulty.

> This year the company had difficulty recruiting sales representatives in the United States.

Read the two sentences aloud or have someone read them to you. Notice how much better and more natural the second sentence sounds. This is for two reasons: First, the words are used as they were meant to be used; that is, the nouns and verbs are used as nouns and verbs, not as modifiers as they are used in the first sentence. Second, the word order is closer to the word order you would use in ordinary conversation.

Writing evolved long after speech. At first it was an attempt to record speech, and to a degree it still is. But anyone who thinks there is little or no difference between writing and speaking is mistaken.

MYTH NUMBER TWO: *Professional writers are so talented that they can just "dash off" a letter, a memo, or an article, turning out perfect copy with little effort.* This is nonsense. Amateurs "dash off" things; professionals take writing too seriously for that. I rewrote the brief foreword to this book at least six times before I was satisfied with it.

The lesson is, if you want to write like a pro, you have to work at it.

MYTH NUMBER THREE: *Writing is a glamorous occupation.* It is true that some writers become rich and famous. Some are even revered, and their names may be immortal. But they are only a handful of the hundreds of thousands of men and women who earn money for writing, including newspaper reporters, house-organ editors, advertising copywriters, speech writers, and public-relations writers. Most of these people would laugh at a suggestion that theirs is a "glamorous" occupation. Most of them would tell you that writing is hard work and not glamorous at all. Satisfying, yes; glamorous, no.

MYTH NUMBER FOUR: *Good writers are "creative" people. Creative* is a word that gives me trouble. I'm not certain what it means. Frankly, I'd rather be described as competent, thoughtful, thorough. I *know* what those words mean. Most writers consider themselves craftsmen, not artists, the title of Kilpatrick's fine book notwithstanding.

MYTH NUMBER FIVE: *Because words are the tools of a writer, you have to have a very large vocabulary if you want to write well.* Many writers, perhaps most, know more words than the typical man or woman in other professions, probably because an interest in words goes with writing. But this doesn't mean that they use all these words when they write. The late Truman Capote is said to have been almost a living dictionary, yet his writing is beautifully simple. Most good writers use only a fraction of the words they know. William F. Buckley, a writer whom I admire immensely, is an exception: His work is best read with a dictionary at hand.

A typical person probably has a working vocabulary of about 10,000 words. He could communicate reasonably well for most purposes with fewer. If two 10,000-word people are talking with (or writing to) each other, each may know a thousand or so words the other doesn't. In such a case there's a potential "understanding gap" of 2,000 words.

For a writer to impart information clearly and efficiently, a huge vocabulary simply isn't needed. Most of us could add both variety and precision to our writing by making better use of words we already know. *Vulnerable,* for example, is a word that you probably know. *Defenseless, exposed,* and *untenable* are related words, and you probably know them as well. But each has a slightly different connotation. The careful writer will be conscious of what different connotations related words have and will choose the word that conveys precisely what he wants to say.

Several years ago I became conscious of a lack of variety in my writing. This was not because I didn't know enough words; it was because I had let myself fall into a rut, which is a self-indulgent way of saying that I had grown lazy. I simply wasn't taking the time to come up with the exact word I needed. As an exercise in self-discipline, I started jotting down serviceable words that I rarely used, and I made a point to use them more often. This exercise did not add one word to my vocabulary, but it added a couple of hundred to my *working* vocabulary.

A good working vocabulary sometimes saves words and eliminates the need for tedious explanations. For example, if I had been unable to use the word *vocabulary* in this discussion, I would have had to use several words in its stead each time.

MYTH NUMBER SIX: *With so many other forms of communication available in business today, writing is less important than it once was.* If that were true, few people would buy books on writing. In *Megatrends,* John Naisbitt wrote, "In this literacy-intensive society . . . we need basic reading and writing skills more than ever before." And Paul Kerins, vice president for human resources for Barnett Banks of Florida, Inc., gave an interview to *The Wall Street Journal* in which he discussed the quality of job applicants. "The one thing we find lacking in college graduates," he said, "is sound writing skills."

A much publicized survey revealed that corporate executives spend 22 percent of their time reading and writing memos. Bad writing can cost a company a lot of money because badly written memos, reports, and other business communications waste time and may cause misunderstanding.

Probably the most compelling reason for writing better is that there is more to read than ever and, for most of us, less time to devote to reading. Anything you write has to compete for attention. The better it is, the better chance it has to win the judgment calls. A century ago, verbosity was not considered as troublesome in writing as it is today, because the pace of business life was more leisurely.

PREFERENCES WRITERS SHARE

Writers come in all sizes and shapes. They write on just about every subject the mind of man can conceive. Their interests vary.

Their backgrounds vary. But most good writers have this in common: They share certain preferences about writing. These preferences are identified by Wilfred Bell and J. G. Stone in *Prose Style*. Most good writers, say Stone and Bell, prefer verbs to nouns, the active voice to the passive voice, the concrete to the abstract, the personal to the impersonal, and the shorter to the longer. I would add that most good writers also prefer the simple to the complex.

Most good writers prefer verbs to nouns. But, you say, a verb is a verb and a noun is a noun. You can't write without using both. Right. But some writers often go out of their way to take a perfectly good verb, which is a strong, active word, and toss it away in favor of a weak noun construction. For example, they might choose *make a decision* rather than the simple, direct *decide*.

Verbs, by definition, are "action words." Using them well is a key to vigorous writing.

Most good writers prefer the active voice to the passive voice. (Note: *Active voice* and *passive voice* are grammatical terms you should know. If you're uncertain what they mean, see Appendix E. *Voice* will be discussed in more detail in Chapter 3.) The passive voice is useful, at times even necessary; but it is less vigorous than the active voice. It sometimes obscures meaning, and it requires more words.

Most good writers prefer concrete words to abstract words, specifics to generalities, the definite to the indefinite, and the direct to the indirect. This does not mean that a good writer never uses an abstract word. It means that a good writer knows that the more abstract a word is — and yes, there *are* degrees of abstraction — the less it says about a subject. If you say, for instance, that *several* things were discussed in a meeting, you leave it to your reader to supply the number. If you say that *eight* things were discussed, you leave no doubt. I call concrete language "the language of control." This is important, and we'll explore it further.

Good writers prefer the personal to the impersonal. Informality is not appropriate in all cases, but most readers are comfortable with a more personal style. At one time teachers cautioned against using the personal pronouns *I* and *me* lest the writer seem egotistical. The admonition gave rise to all sorts of awkward alternatives to *I* — *the undersigned, this writer, myself,* and even *we.* Today we need not hesitate to use *I, me, you,* and other personal pronouns in most kinds of writing. Excessive use of *I* or *me* is still to be avoided, however.

Good writers prefer shorter to longer. They like shorter words, shorter sentences, shorter paragraphs. Good writers are word misers; they don't like to take ten words to say what they could say in five. They respect words too much to misuse or overuse them. Some good writers do write long sentences, but they construct their sentences so skillfully that they don't seem long.

Good writers prefer the simple to the complex. Showoffs like to make things more complicated than they need to be. Perhaps they get a sense of power from writing something the unwashed masses can't comprehend. Good writers like to use their skills to make things understandable. I wonder where toy makers find those characters they hire to write directions for assembling toys.

These are preferences that most good writers share. The *whys* of the preferences are the essence of this book.

THE FIVE C'S OF GOOD WRITING

A simple, but effective, way to judge writing is to apply the criteria known as the Five C's. I don't know the origin of the Five C's. I've seen them several times in one form or another. They are:

Clear
Correct — fact ⟵ mechanic (grammer)
Complete
Concise
Considerate

Good writing is clear. If business writing isn't clear, it is useless at best. At worst, it can cost a company money, damage its reputation, and alienate customers. What does it take to ensure clarity? Good word usage, good grammar, proper punctuation, and good sentence structure are important, but they alone cannot guarantee a sentence will be understandable. Consider, for instance, the following excerpt from an article on house organs, written by an alleged professional:

> Today, in an increasingly mobile, tormented, and fragmented society, the role and purpose of a company publication is to build a silhouette of pertinence and to make effective contributions

toward moderation across a protean spectrum of a corporation's public. The result is good business!

Have you any idea of what that means? I haven't; and I guess I've read it a hundred times. Nevertheless, I can't fault the grammar, the punctuation, or the sentence structure. All I know is, if the result of all that is "good business," I've been misguided about business practices. Try the following for contrast:

> I seed the man runned out from the bank. He war big and he wear overhalls. He ain't no more than ten or fifteen yard fore he trip and fall and them cops hop rite on hem.

Any doubt about what the writer of that passage saw? Bad grammar, bad spelling, bad syntax? Yes. Unclear? No. I don't condone bad grammar, bad spelling, and bad syntax. But asked to choose between the two passages, I'd take the second without hesitating. The writer of the first, who presumably took money for that misbegotten gibberish, was showing off; the writer of the second was communicating.

Good writing is correct. The information it presents is accurate, and it is free of errors in grammar, spelling, and punctuation.

Good writing is complete. Is anything more exasperating than to receive a memo, a letter, or a sheet of instructions for assembling some contraption only to find that you haven't been given all the information you need in order to do what you're supposed to do?

Good writing is concise. It is free of redundancies and superfluous details. It gives enough information, but no more than necessary. It is long enough to accomplish its purpose, but no longer. Later in the book we'll work on making your writing more concise.

Good writing is considerate. It doesn't waste the reader's time or impugn his intelligence. It is meant to *inform,* not to *impress.* (Do you suppose the writer of the passage about company publications was trying to impress someone with his vocabulary?) Considerate writing is free of thoughtless or intentional language that might be taken as racist or sexist.

The Five C's are a good way to judge business writing. Come to think of it, if writing is clear, complete, correct, concise, and considerate, it is also reader-friendly.

EXERCISE 1: JUDGING BY THE FIVE C'S

The passages below were extracted from documents prepared by representatives of a huge financial institution. Judge them by the criteria of The Five C's. If you think they fail to meet any of the criteria, edit or rewrite them. Then take a look at my comments (Appendix A) and see how your versions compare with mine.

Example Number One: The subject neighborhood, within a 1 mile radius of the property, has an average household income of $44,200 and a medium home value of over $76,000. Within the same radius approximately 72% of the employment base hold managerial, sales and/or administrative support positions.

Example Number Two: As additional participation interest, the company shall receive the greater of $4,500,000 or 50% of the sale proceeds or net equity value, above the loan balance upon sale of the property to a bona fide third party, at loan maturity, or at refinancing the project. Net equity value represents the total value as determined by sale or appraisal, less the following: 1) actual costs of sale (not to exceed 3%) and 2) the loan balance, excluding any deferred interest.

Example Number Three: The primary risk associated with this transaction is that the property will be unable to achieve and continue to obtain stabilized proforma occupancy and generate the expected income necessary to support the company's debt service.

Example Number Four: The primary risk in this project is the property's failure to lease-up to breakeven occupancy. The risk is mitigated by the high occupancy in the competing projects of 95%, and the appropriate mix of apartments of 10 studios, the most difficult units to rent with the highest vacancy, to 110 one-bedroom units, to 31 two-bedrooms. This risk is further mitigated by the experience of the borrower team, which includes The Crossing, a highly respected management team specializing in elderly housing facilities primarily in the West.

A SAMPLER OF GOOD WRITING

Often I am asked to give examples of *good* writing. Frankly, I much prefer to give examples of *bad* writing because I usually have no trouble explaining why bad writing is bad. Errors of grammar, syntax, and word use are easy to spot, and I can use them to support my opinions. Good writing, however, is a different matter. Defending an opinion on something that subjective isn't easy. Nevertheless, I offer you the following examples of writing that is, in my opinion, good. The selections are from a variety of sources.

The first is from an article by Ezra Bowen in the March 1988 issue of *Smithsonian* magazine. It's about two blizzards that hit Nebraska and the Dakota Territory on January 12, 1888:

> Little Charley Bard, a Nebraska boy of 8 or 9, got caught at the far edge of a furrowed cornfield beside his school. Wind and whirling sleet knocked him to the earth, where he lay, unable to get up or open his eyes. With a country boy's presence of mind, he started to worm his way along the ground, groping from one furrow to another, taking his direction from the set of the ragged corn rows. After perhaps 20 minutes that must have seemed like many hours, Charley bumped into the side of the school building, felt along to the door and pounded till it was jerked open and he tumbled inside.

The next selection is from *The Lessons of History*, by Will and Ariel Durant, scholars of impeccable credentials.

> History is subject to geology. Every day the sea encroaches somewhere upon the land, or the land upon the sea; cities disappear under the water, and cathedrals ring their melancholy bells. Mountains rise and fall in the rhythms of emergence and erosion; rivers swell and flood, or dry up, or change their course; valleys become deserts, and isthmuses become straits. To the geologic eye all the surface of earth is a fluid form, and man moves upon it as insecurely as Peter walking on the waves to Christ.

This is from Truman Capote's short story "A Tree of Night":

> It was winter. A string of naked bulbs, from which it seemed all warmth had been drained, illuminated the little depot's cold, windy platform. Earlier in the evening it had rained, and now icicles hung along the station-house eaves like some crystal monster's teeth. Except for a girl, the platform was deserted. The girl wore a gray flannel suit, a raincoat, and a plaid scarf. Her hair, parted in the middle and rolled up neatly on the sides, was rich blondish brown; and, while her face tended to be too thin and narrow, she was, though not extraordinarily so, attractive.

From the Spring 1988 catalogue of Austad's, a company that sells golf equipment:

We're proud of our new EZ18 Golf Bag. Quite simply, it's the most convenient, comfortable carry bag we've ever seen — and we'd think so even if we hadn't designed this one ourselves. We've packed this bag with all the features golfers ask for — beginning with the full-length nylon club-dividers that save wear and tear on grips and shafts.

An advertising slogan for Coca-Cola that was used during the 1960s:

Coke has the taste you never get tired of.

From John Steinbeck's *America and the Americans.*

Kirk dressed in a blue shirt and overalls like most farmers, but he left his orchard only once a week. On Saturday he came to a little feed store my father owned and bought ten cents' worth of middlings — about five pounds, I suppose. Middlings were simply ground wheat with the chaff left in; it would be called whole wheat now, but then it was sold for chicken and pig feed. His weekly purchase was remarkable because the Kirks had neither chickens nor pigs. Mrs. Kirk and the daughter were rarely seen. They never left the orchard, but we could peer through the black cypress hedge which surrounded the orchard and see two gaunt, gray women, so much alike that you couldn't tell which was mother and which was daughter. As far as anyone knew, the ten cents' worth of middings was all Mr. Kirk ever bought. First the daughter faded and sickened and died, and soon after, Mrs. Kirk went the same way. The coroner said they starved to death; we would call it malnutrition now – but there was no evidence of violence. People did mind their own business then. But I do know that after they died, Mr. Kirk bought five cents' worth of middlings a week.

From the 1988 annual report of Equifax Inc.:

Equifax provides a number of informational services to help customers sell their products more efficiently. Marketing research is an example.

Equifax's marketing research affiliate is one of the nation's most prestigious. Working with a list of clients that includes some of the best known names in American business, our marketing research professionals conduct sophisticated studies to determine consumer attitudes toward products and services.

From a letter to Abigail Van Buren:

DEAR ABBY: I am a third-grader at Marion Street School in Lynbrook, N. Y. Our teacher, Mr. Freifeld, took the class down to the lunchroom to find out how many students threw out their lunches. . . .

First, we found out how many kids ate in the lunchroom every day. There were 252. Then we looked in the garbage cans and counted the whole sandwiches that were thrown out. There were 39 untouched sandwiches, still in their wrappers. There were 30 half-sandwiches still wrapped. Peanut butter and jelly was thrown out the most!

We figured that almost one out of every four people threw away all or half their lunch. With people starving all over the world, that is a lot of food to waste. It was enough to make you sick.

We counted the drinks, too. We found 22 whole containers of drink thrown out. Some were milk, but most were juice.

There was a whole pile of fruit — apples, oranges and bananas — that was thrown into the garbage. Good grapes, too.

Our class decided that maybe the parents should ask their kids what they want for lunch, then maybe the kids wouldn't throw out so much. Thank you. — Clayton Cohn, N. Y.

Finally, casting modesty aside, I offer an excerpt from my short story, "The Oracle of Screven County":

We were talking baseball the day he made his first prediction. I can just see him sitting on the bank of Brier Creek, leaning against a big tree, fishing pole tucked under his arm, his sweat-marked old hat pulled down over his eyes. . . .

Not long after that they wrote up Uncle Mac in *The Sylvania Telephone*. A man with baggy pants and pockets full of flash bulbs took his picture with a big camera and asked a bunch of silly questions like had he ever thought of playing the stock market. Uncle Mac tried his best to be funny. When the man asked about clairvoyance, Uncle Mac said the only *Claire* he ever knew was a waitress down at the cafe that married a feller Mock that farmed over near Po' Robin and he couldn't recall her maiden name though he was pretty sure it wasn't anything like Voyance.

If these diverse passages are samples of good writing, what do they have in common that makes them good? First, they are simple and direct; they can be readily understood by anyone. I would be surprised if all the passages together contained more than two words not in the everyday vocabulary of everyone who reads this book. It seems in a way remarkable that eminent historians, famous novelists, a writer of magazine articles, an unknown ad copywriter, an obscure writer of catalogue copy, a writer of financial reports, and a third-grade student should share this ability to write simply and directly even when their writing styles are so different.

The second thing these samples have in common is that they all do what they are supposed to do. Notice how effectively the third-grader, Clayton Cohn, uses specific language ("30 untouched sandwiches," "22 whole cartons of drink") to make his case. Whether writing "makes its case" may be what counts most.

EXERCISE 2: WRITING A BUSINESS MEMO

Imagine that you are communications director of a large national company that provides special services to the insurance industry. Your company has changed the name of one of its services. Your assignment is to write a memorandum announcing this change to the company's field force — the men and women who call on customers, make sales presentations, and perform the service. Their acceptance of the change is important.

You decide what information is pertinent and how the memo should be organized. As you write, remember the Five C's. Consider the following information:

1. Old name of service: Possible Duplicate Coverage Report. New name: Coordination of Benefits Report.

2. What the service does: Basically, the service helps to identify situations in which a health-insurance policyholder is covered by more than one insurance company, as when a husband or a wife is covered under the other spouse's group plan. That's how the name Possible Duplicate Coverage Report came about. "Coordination of benefits" is a term used in the insurance industry to describe what happens when duplicate coverage exists. The two companies usually "coordinate" — that is, each pays a portion of the claim so that the claimant does not make a profit from the accident or illness. It probably helps hold down insurance costs.

3. Although "possible duplicate coverage" is a descriptive term, "coordination of benefits" is more customer-oriented because it is a term that is common in the insurance industry. Before

making the change, the company surveyed some of its customers in the United States. In that survey, 97 percent said they preferred "Coordination of Benefits Report" to "Possible Duplicate Coverage Report." Presumably, they felt more comfortable with a name that reflects industry terminology.

4. With the new name, the company must revise all pertinent forms. One form, number 18905, has already been revised, and you are reproducing it on the reverse of your memo in order to show the field people what the new forms will look like. Others will be revised eventually.

5. Nothing about the service has been changed except the name. It will be performed, handled, billed, and promoted as usual.

6. The company wants everyone to begin using the new name as soon as possible.

By the end of the book, you'll have four versions of the same memo: the one you will write, the one the company sent, an edited version of the company's memo, and my version of the company memo.

2.
Put Your Writing on a Diet

Writing improves in direct ratio to the
number of things we can keep out of it
that shouldn't be there.
— William Zinsser, *On Writing Well*

Anyone who writes ought to keep William Zinsser's words in a gilt frame on the office wall. Much writing, probably *most* business writing, is a-clutter with excess words that rob it of vitality and efficiency. Sentences huff and puff like an overweight man trying to jog uphill. "Businessese" clogs the communications arteries that lead to the heart of a corporation. Corporations, it seems, rarely just *do* something; they do it *successfully* — or *effectively.* And no self-respecting middle manager trying to impress the boss would write such a simple word as *use,* because *utilize* is so much more, well, corporate.

Now, of course, there is nothing glaringly wrong with utilizing *utilize.* But the word seems to symbolize a malaise that afflicts many business people when they sit down to write. The prevailing symptom is an uncontrollable urge always to use a long word when a short one will serve as well. Writers so afflicted also are convinced that two words are more effective than one even if the second word adds not a modicum of meaning nor a tinge of enlightenment.

Many business people believe that the more words they use to express themselves the more emphasis they give to their ideas. The converse is closer to the truth: The more a reader has to concentrate on, the less attention he can give to any single idea.

Wilson Follett, one of the foremost authorities on usage, had this to say in his book, *Modern American Usage:*

> ... [T]o eliminate the vice of wordiness is to ensure the virtue of emphasis, which depends more on conciseness than on any other factor. Wherever we can make twenty-five words do the work of fifty, we halve the area in which looseness and disorganization can flourish, and by reducing the span of attention required we increase the force of thought. To make our words count for as much as possible is surely the simplest as well as the hardest secret of style.

Almost everyone who writes a business communication writes to impress someone or to obtain someone's approval. Approvals from several layers of the corporate hierarchy may be required for a communication of consequence. When making a favorable impression on someone is uppermost in a writer's mind, the temptation is to use the most "impressive" (read that "long") words he can think of. Many bright young men and women capable of writing clearly and concisely never get a chance to show it when they work for a large corporation. A woman in one of my seminars was pleasantly surprised when I told her I would prefer *use* to *utilize.* She explained that every time she wrote *use* her boss would change it to *utilize* before he would send the communication to his boss. She told me she was beginning to think she was wrong to use such a simple word.

If you're the boss, you're lucky; nobody is going to change what you write. But if you're not the boss, chances are someone a floor or so above will be your editor. Be warned: If you start to write better, not everyone is going to be comfortable with the results.

A friend, the public relations director of a large company, confessed to me that he often uses pompous language and corporate jargon when he writes something that has to go upstairs for approval. "It's the only way I can be sure to get it past top management," he said.

My daughter, who learned respect for words before she learned to walk, did some consulting work for a large company. Part of her assignment was to interview executives, determine exactly what they did, and write job descriptions. She described one marketing executive's primary responsibility as "planning sales promotions." On review, the executive insisted it be changed to "planning, developing, and implementing the execution of marketing and other promotional programs and activities."

Whew!

Those anecdotes illustrate a common business attitude: If something is simple, it doesn't sound important, and if it doesn't *sound* important, it can't *be* important. An executive who is more comfortable with simple language than with "bafflegab" is a rare specimen in business today.

When you begin to write clearly and simply, you're almost certain to make some people uncomfortable. But you'll never be misunderstood. And you might be lucky enough to have a boss with the insight of Franklin D. Roosevelt. President Roosevelt, a man who could do marvelous things with words, had little patience with the ponderous prose of government memos. One such memo, written by a White House staffer in 1942, managed to turn what should have been a simple directive into a missive that only a bureaucrat could love:

> Such preparations shall be made as will completely obscure all Federal buildings and non-Federal buildings occupied by the Federal government during an air raid for any period of time from visibility by reason of internal or external illumination.

Does the style sound familiar? The turkey who wrote that one probably thought it was impressive. The President wasn't impressed; he ordered it rewritten. "Tell them," he said, "that in buildings where they have to keep the work going to put something across the windows."

More people in business, government, and the professions are coming to recognize the value of clear writing. In 1979, *Fortune* magazine asked executives what they thought business schools should stress. Many answered, "better writing." More and more businesses are insisting that their employees learn to write better. My one-day seminar has attracted men and women from many large companies. One company engaged me to give seminars to almost eighty people. Every bookstore has a selection of books on writing. Former TV network superstar Edwin Newman draws big crowds to his lectures on the deplorable state of English usage.

Even lawyers are getting in on the act. Some of the big law firms and state and local bar associations sponsor seminars to teach lawyers to write clearly without sacrificing legal precision. At least one state supreme court (Georgia) has a full-time writing consultant whose mission is to translate the court's opinions into understandable English. And William O. Rehnquist, in his first week as chief justice of the United States, earned my undying admiration when he called down an attorney for using the non-word *irregardless*. Somebody cares!

All this gives hope that some day good writing will be the rule rather than the exception in America's corporations and among its respected professionals.

Probably the most important step you can take to improve your writing is to get rid of the fat. This chapter will tell you *how* to do it, and I hope it will convince you that it's worth doing. Seminar participants have told me that they have become addicted to fat-cutting, not only in their writing, but in the writing of others.

DON'T OVERUSE ADJECTIVES AND ADVERBS

William Strunk and E. B. White, authors of *The Elements of Style,* offer some good advice:

> Write with nouns and verbs, not adjectives and adverbs. The adjective has not been built that can pull a weak or inaccurate noun out of a tight place.

Not all writers take that advice. They should; their writing would be better.

A news release from a large Southern university, a school with high standards, reports that "The ensemble concertizes constantly throughout [the state] and performs informative concerts to thousands of school children." Even if we could accept the invented verb, *concertize,* which I am informed is common among musicians, I'd have to question whether *constantly* and *informative* add to the thought. The sentence is fat. What's wrong with "The ensemble performs for school children throughout [the state]"? The release goes on to describe the ensemble's artistic director as "an *active* composer-performer." (My emphasis.)

Is it possible, I wonder, to be an *in*active composer-performer? Well, maybe. If the point was worth making, it was worth a few words of explanation.

Many adjectives and adverbs can be omitted without sacrificing anything important. And when they can be, they should be. Words such as *constantly, informative,* and *active,* as they are used in the example, usually are evidence of a writer's lack of confidence in strong, simple words. Well-chosen nouns and verbs rarely need the intensification adjectives and adverbs are supposed to provide. *Perform,* for example, evokes an active image, but *concertize* (Yuk!) tiptoes around the subject and seems to require *constantly* to make its point.

Another news release, this one touting an excellent restaurant, offers this gem: "LaTour's beauty and grandeur combined with the culinary artistry of Executive Chef Charles Toth and the front-of-the-house expertise of Serge Renard and Jean Pierre Abraham, makes [sic] LaTour ready to take it's [sic] place among the memorable and celebrated dining establishments in the country." Reading LaTour's self-description is enough to give you indigestion. A restaurant that good deserves a palatable news release.

And, a letter from the superintendent of a metropolitan school system advocates "a more supportive and reciprocal alliance with this noteworthy venture" to provide scholarships.

Even professional writers contribute to word pollution with an effluent of modifiers. A book review in *The Atlanta Journal and Constitution* contained this paragraph:

> But the Reid family never learned how to deal with *The New York Times,* its stately rival for the carriage trade. While the *Times* became evermore solid, largely through the wise reinvestment of its profits, the *Herald Tribune,* first under Helen's older son Whitie, who was signally lacking in leadership ability, and then her brash, energetic second son Brown, floundered embarrassingly through a succession of meager efforts, such as a doomed Early Bird edition, and a beneath-its-dignity puzzle contest called Tangle Towns, to save the paper.

Leaves you breathless, doesn't it?

Adverbs contribute even more to bloated prose than adjectives do. *Successfully, actually, totally,* and *effectively* are almost always redundant. I sometimes challenge seminar participants to use *successfully* without being redundant. Most attempts are unsuccessful. Expressions like *blared loudly* and *willingly agreed* are so common they scarcely elicit a chuckle. They deserve a hoot.

Knowing the value of understatement and harboring a distaste for overstatement, good writers seldom use such superlatives as *terrific, wonderful, marvelous,* and *fantastic.* They prefer to give facts and let the reader supply the adjectives. Besides, conversational overuse of those words has rendered them all but meaningless.

Carefully chosen and sparingly used, adjectives and adverbs can serve a writer well. But they should be considered guilty until proven innocent — guilty of making your writing fat and sluggish.

Try this: Select a sample of business writing — three or four paragraphs from a corporate annual report will do — and strike out *all* adjectives and adverbs. Then read the edited copy and ask yourself whether you have omitted anything important. If so, restore the words that seem necessary. Chances are you'll have a stronger piece of writing. Doing that kind of editing is easy with another person's writing. The test comes when you try it with your own.

LET NOUNS BE NOUNS

Any good craftsman knows what happens when you try to use a tool to do a job it wasn't designed to do: The job isn't done right, and the tool might be damaged. And a good writer knows that each part of speech has a purpose. When one part of speech is asked to do the work of another, the results likely will be unsatisfactory. Take the lamentable practice of converting nouns into adjectives.

I don't recall hearing the TV weatherman forecast rain recently; but we've had a lot of *shower activity.* Old-fashioned crises never come up anymore, but we encounter an inordinate number of *crisis situations.* And who wants to face up to the fact that the city has slums when *slum areas* are so much easier to accept?

These and other examples of nouns modifying other nouns are common in business writing. Lawyers and engineers especially are fond of "adjectivizing" nouns, and writers of business documents often adopt the practice to give their writing a pseudo-technical or psuedo-legal cast.

Turning nouns into adjectives doesn't violate any rule. In fact, it is standard in phrases like *school children, kitchen cabinet,* and *government official.* But those expressions serve a purpose. For example, *kitchen* tells us the writer is referring to a cabinet that's installed in a kitchen, not a bathroom. To my knowledge, there's no other way to say it without using several words. *Shower activity,* however, tells us nothing more than *showers* or *rain.*

An article on suburban development points out that "The utilities and transportation infrastructure have not kept pace with commercial development." Aside from the fact that the singular subject, *infrastructure,* requires the verb *has,* the sentence complicates a simple concept by using *infrastructure,* which requires "adjectivized" nouns to explain what it means. *Utilities and transportation* is less burdensome to the reader than *utilities and transportation infrastructure.*

Ronald Goldfarb and James C. Raymond, in *Clear Understandings,* a guide to legal writing, deplore the practice of converting nouns into adjectives. They also deplore "noun chains" — strings of nouns modifying each other. Goldfarb and Raymond call noun chains "ugly and pretentious." They point out that noun chains place an unnecessary burden on a reader.

If you want to find examples of noun chains, corporate financial communications are a likely source. The quarterly report of an oil company is replete with such clumsy phrases as *oil and gas liquids sales, oil and gas exploration costs,* and *products profit margins.* Another company's quarterly report laments the "United States sales representative recruiting difficulty." Still another tells its shareholders that the chief executive has appointed "an automation hardware selection team."

Constructing noun chains is sometimes defended as a way to save words; and of course it is true that all but one of the examples cited above require fewer words than their alternatives. (Example: *costs of exploring for oil and gas* instead of *oil and gas exploration costs.*) But the saving of words in these cases is false economy. Its cost is clarity and grace. Although most good writers are word misers, none will hesitate to use an extra word or two when doing so will make a sentence clearer or more natural.

Oil and gas exploration costs has only five words; *costs of exploring for oil and gas* has seven. To me, the alternative seems shorter. It is without question easier to read.

BEWARE OF "INSTANT REDUNDANCIES"

Some words usually cannot be modified without creating a redundancy. Nevertheless, writers addicted to fat can't seem to resist the temptation to add modifiers where none is needed. I call this practice creating instant redundancies. *Unique*, for example, is seen often with a useless appendage such as *very*, *totally*, or *somewhat*. Unique means one of a kind. Nothing can be more unique or less unique.

Could is another example. Could should never be accompanied by *possibly*. *Perfect* means perfect, and that's as far as you can go. Much as I admire the Constitution of the United States, I would prefer that it had been ordained to form "a perfect union" or "a stronger union" rather than "a more perfect union." All things considered, I suppose we can forgive Thomas Jefferson for one instant redundancy.

DROWN YOUR BABIES

It isn't as gruesome as it sounds. "Drown your babies" was advice old-time editors used to give to young reporters. And it scarcely could be expressed better. It was the editors' way of telling their charges to take a heavy pencil and strike out some of those useless words and phrases and inappropriate metaphors they had so proudly birthed.

Writers today could do with that kind of advice. This includes me. I often have reread a passage I have written, only to find things in it that sounded like hell. Funny thing is, I loved them when I wrote them.

Editing your own writing takes self-discipline, but if you don't have an editor handy, you have to do it yourself. Be brutal; drown those babies.

SIMPLIFY, SIMPLIFY

Usually in my writing seminar I give the participants this sentence and ask them how it can be simplified:

At this particular point in time, the company is almost bankrupt.

Almost immediately someone will suggest eliminating *particular*. Then another will chime in with "What's wrong with *at this time?*" After a few more suggestions, someone almost always will make the point that *now* can substitute for *at this particular point in time.*

That's when I hold up a sheet that looks like this:

AT THIS PARTICULAR POINT IN TIME
AT THIS PARTICULAR TIME
AT THIS POINT IN TIME
AT THE PRESENT TIME
AT THE PRESENT
AT THIS POINT
AT PRESENT
PRESENTLY
NOW
IS

Of course. *Is* says it all. *The company is almost bankrupt.*

Good writers almost always opt for the short, simple way of saying something. When they don't, they have good reasons. For example, in the sentence that began this discussion, there could be a reason to use *now* or even the more wordy *at this point.* Suppose the writer wanted to compare the company's current financial condition with its condition of a month earlier. In such a case, the sentence might read, "Last month the company seemed to be recovering, but at this point it is almost bankrupt."

The difference is, a good writer uses extra words to created a desired effect. A fat-loving writer throws in extra words for no particular reason — unless it's to give his opinions a little added weight. Pun intended.

As publications manager for The Coca-Cola Company some years ago, I had on my staff a woman fresh from journalism school. She was bright, and she obviously had been trained in the craft of fat-free writing. The trouble was, she had adopted a writing style that was *too* sparse. She was one of the few writers I've known who really needed to be less of a word miser. I told her so, but she refused to accept my judgment until I came up with an analogy that she could relate to. You may find it meaningful.

The difference between prime beef and the lower grades — other than the cost — is that prime beef has more fat. It's not a lot more; it's just enough to make the meat tenderer and tastier. Beef that's not "marbled" with fat is just as nutritious, but it doesn't taste as good. My advice to her was to add a bit of fat here and there for "flavor."

For most of us, however, the problem is too much fat. My advice to you — unless you're exceptional — is to trim your writing to the essentials. Then you might add a few words that, strictly speaking, could be omitted. Emphasis, pacing, and flavor are important to good writing.

EXERCISE 3: SIMPLIFY

Simplify the following sentences without changing their meaning.

1. You'll find the answers listed on page 32.

2. A good salesman will make approximately four to six calls on a daily basis.

3. Margaret Mitchell achieved a considerable degree of personal fame as a result of the success of her best-selling fiction novel, *Gone With the Wind.*

4. There were a number of things that were discussed by us at the meeting yesterday.

5. The car is available in three different colors. They are red, white, and blue.

6. Here for your perusal is a complete listing of all medical doctors of the area in and around the city of Philadelphia.

7. There is no easy shortcut to expressing yourself well by means of the written word.

8. This book, which was published very recently, contains a very great deal of accurate, truthful, and up-to-date factual information.

9. We are in receipt of your recent letter in which you offered your resignation from the club. We are indeed sorry that you feel it necessary to take this very regrettable action at this particular point in time when the club is already short of members.

10. The company was very supportive of each and every person who voiced an objection to the newly enacted rules and regulations.

EXERCISE 4: BOIL IT DOWN

Another piece of advice once prevalent in newsrooms was "boil it down until it sizzles." This chapter, "Put Your Writing on a Diet," is about how to make your business letters, memos, reports, and other communications sizzle by getting rid of the fat. As your writing improves, you'll find you're putting in fewer unnecessary words. Even so, you'll have plenty of chances to remove fat when you edit your work or the work of others. In this exercise, you'll get the chance to do a number on someone else's writing.

Below is the text of a letter that a company president drafted to send to clients and potential clients. Fortunately, he had the good sense to ask his public relations counselor to look it over. It was never sent.

See how much fat you can remove from it by editing. Don't do any rewriting, except where you have to supply a word or two to substitute for material you take out. Don't try to make judgments about the content; that's Mr. Doe's prerogative.

Dear _____:

One of the more interesting aspects about life here in Savannah over the past few years has been the change of pace associated with its health care delivery systems. In the past 12 months alone, 5 Health Maintenance Organizations have opened their doors and 3 Preferred Provider Organizations have been established to cite but two developments. One result: employers such as yourself are today confronted with more options than ever in the ongoing battle to reduce health care benefit costs.

It is within this context that I am writing to update you on MediHealth's progress. In light of our continued growth, I plan to follow up this letter with additional updates about Medi-Health.

Let me begin by reporting that since January 1 of this year, we have increased our membership by approximately 32 percent, giving us a total of over 3,000 members throughout our 13-county service area.

We believe that the single biggest reason for our growth and progress in Savannah has been that, beyond reducing employer health care costs, MediHealth actually has been able to deliver quality health care without cutting corners. In fact, we continue to get positive feedback from our members about the comprehensive benefits and services we offer. We take great pride in knowing that our commitment to quality health care is recognized and appreciated by our members.

Since its founding 18 months ago, MediHealth has evolved into the nation's largest independent investor-owned operation of HMOs. Today it operates ___ HMOs in ___ states, which collectively serve an enrollee population in excess of ___

Savannah's health care picture will continue to change, rapidly as the balance of the 1980s unfolds. But MediHealth's perspective is long-term: We seek to serve the community well by contributing to the so-called quality of life here in the most intelligent and consistent manner possible. We envision doing this not only by delivering quality health care at an affordable cost, but also by broadening our preventive health care for our members.

HMOs are not the sole answer in the ongoing health care "riddle," but HMOs do represent one of several useful alternatives to employers seeking to offer a reasonable array of health benefits to their employees with high-quality care and with no financial surprises. Thus, to the extent that you may be re-examining your health benefit situation, we would appreciate an opportunity to meet with you to learn first-hand what your particular health care concerns and needs are, and then to respond with what we trust will be a thoughtful proposal for your consideration.

On behalf of Medi-Health, our many thanks for your interest and attention.

Sincerely,

Joe Doe

3.
Put Energy into Your Writing

[M]ake your words forceful, compact, and ener-
getic. . . . A few strong, carefully selected words
will deliver your message with the kick of a mule.
— Mark S. Bacon, *Write Like the Pros*

Never having been kicked by a mule, I'm unable to vouch for the suitability of Mr. Bacon's metaphor. Nevertheless, I understand and appreciate the sentiment behind it. Reader-friendly writing is energetic writing, and energetic writing is fat-free. Just as an overweight person often lacks energy, a sentence with excess verbiage cannot move briskly along from one thought to the next. But a *thin* person can lack energy. So can writing that is not grossly fat. Poorly chosen words, improper use of verbs, and weak sentence structure can rob your writing of its energy.

PASSIVE V. ACTIVE

Because a verb is the "power plant" of a sentence, learning to use verbs well is the first step in putting energy into your writing.

In grammar, *voice* refers to the relationship of a verb to its subject. If the subject of a verb is the *doer* of the action, the sentence is in the *active* voice. If the subject is the *receiver* of the action, the sentence is in the *passive* voice. Stated another way, the difference is whether the subject *acts* (Frankie shot Johnny.) or is *acted upon* (Johnny was shot by Frankie.). An easy way to remember this is to think of the cliché, "Don't put the cart before the horse." **The horse pulled the cart** is active voice because the subject (horse) of the verb (pulled) did the pulling. Put the cart before the horse and you get **The cart was pulled by the horse,** which is the passive voice because the subject (cart) was pulled.

Note that the active example uses only five words, but the passive uses seven. That's 40 percent more. If you add 40 percent more words to everything you write, your writing will grow to be an intolerable burden on your reader's time and patience. Note also that the active sentence is more energetic.

So one way to put energy in your writing is to make greater use of the active voice. A cart with the horse behind it won't go anywhere.

I once had a teacher who said the passive voice should *never* be used. He was wrong. The passive is useful, even necessary in many instances. Consider how you would change **The criminal was arrested, tried, convicted, and sentenced — all within one month** from the passive to the active voice. It would have to be something like **The police arrested the criminal, a jury tried and convicted him, and a judge sentenced him — all within one month.** Clearly, the passive version is better. It requires fewer words, and it conveys to the reader a feeling of the speed with which the arrest, trial, conviction, and sentencing took place. It also has natural rhythm lacking in the active sentence.

The passive voice sometimes can add a touch of modesty where modesty might be needed, or it can effect a subtle change of emphasis. For example, **We brought the project in under budget** differs from **The project was brought in under budget.** The former (active) stresses *we;* the latter (passive) stresses *project.* Although the sentences have the same number of words, the active *seems* shorter and more vigorous. Note also that no person is involved in the passive sentence. In examples like this, the writer should be guided by the impression he wants to give the reader.

The passive voice can be used to mask or divide responsibility. For example, **Taxes were increased five times in the past five years** is not quite the same as **Congress increased taxes five times in the past five years.** Your pocketbook can't tell the difference, but the passive sentence seems to let Congress off the hook. That's fine, if the writer wants to go easy on the tax-raisers.

Good writers are not slavishly devoted to the active voice. They use either the active or the passive, depending upon what they want to say and how they want the reader to react. Generally, however, they prefer the active. They know that active-voice sentences are usually more vigorous, simpler, and more direct. Passive-voice sentences can be more subtle, but they are slower-paced.

DELETE THOSE EXPLETIVES

A grammatical expletive is a word that temporarily takes the place of the subject or object of a verb. An example is more understandable than the definition. In **It is believed that this book will help you to write better,** *it* is an expletive. In **There are few people who cannot improve their writing,** *there* is an expletive. An expletive is sometimes called a "dummy subject."

Americans became conscious of the word *expletive* during the Nixon-Watergate era. Before releasing transcripts of the infamous Watergate tapes, the government bowdlerized them by substituting *expletive deleted* for presidential profanities. Thus the world will never know whether Mr. Nixon cussed imaginatively or whether his expletives were as ordinary as Mrs. Nixon's Republican cloth coat.

In any case, a grammatical expletive, far from being profane, is welcome in polite society. It is less welcome, however, in lively prose. Expletive constructions slow down writing, and good writers delete as many of them as they can without resorting to awkward phrases.

Expletives cannot be eliminated altogether. How else could you say, *It is raining? The rain is falling* is a bit too poetic for ordinary conversation. It could earn you some strange looks, since rain has never been known to rise.

Even so, eliminating expletives is worth a try. Too many expletive constructions, like too many uses of the passive voice, result in sluggish, monotonous prose. Expletives are favored by the same writers who like to convert verbs to nouns. Something in their nature makes them resist direct statements. The thoughts expressed by the examples in the opening paragraph of this section could be written with fewer words and greater impact as, **This book will help you write better,** and **Most people can improve their writing.**

Certain uses of indefinite pronouns — for example, *they* in

They say falling in love is wonderful — have much the same effect on writing that expletives have. Don't use indefinite pronouns in that way if you can find another way to say what you mean.

EXERCISE 5: PASSIVES AND EXPLETIVES

The purpose of this exercise is to make sure you understand the difference between passive and active voice and that you recognize expletive constructions. Rewrite the sentences below to eliminate expletives and passive-voice constructions. Although this might seem simple, many of my seminar participants had difficulty with these concepts until they were given some practice of this type.

1. It said in the annual report that three new directors were elected by the shareholders this year.

2. It is sunny but cold today.

3. There was little demand for the product, so it was removed from inventory.

4. There was cold chicken in the refrigerator. I ate it, and it was delicious.

5. It is said that the number thirteen is unlucky.

6. It is worth noting that there are three models available.

7. The dog had been beaten unmercifully, but it was treated by the veterinarian who was there by chance.

8. There was much fear of espionage during World War II, even though there was little chance that America would be invaded by the Germans.

9. There is no money in this year's budget for salary increases.

10. "There you go again," Reagan said.

LET VERBS BE VERBS

Writers who are uncomfortable with simple, direct statements love weak verbs, and they regularly convert verbs to nouns. For example, the direct, simple verb *decide* becomes *make a deci-*

sion. Such verb-to-noun conversions are the equivalent of going in by the back door when the front door is closer. Moreover, they rob sentences of their vitality. *Take action, bring to a conclusion, find a solution, make a determination,* and *reach an agreement* are back-door ways of saying *act, conclude, solve, determine,* and *agree.* Such constructions should be used sparingly. Like the passive voice, they are less vigorous than their alternatives. Unlike the passive, they have few redeeming virtues.

Try this: Select an example of business writing several paragraphs long. Underline all the words that end in **-ion, -ing, -ment, -ance,** and **-ence.** Often these endings indicate "backdoor" writing. When that is the case, get rid of them and substitute "front-door" constructions. Then read the material again and note how much more vigorous it sounds.

William Zinsser deplores the use of "concept nouns." In bad writing, concept nouns are used instead of verbs that tell what somebody did. Sentences that use such nouns are "dead sentences." They don't have any people in them. As an example Zinsser cites, **The common reaction is incredulous laughter.** He suggests **Most people just laugh with disbelief** as the better way to say it. His alternative is a sentence about living, breathing, laughing people. It allows readers to participate in the sentence. A reader can visualize people laughing; and when a reader visualizes, he becomes an equal partner in the communication.

VARY SENTENCE LENGTH

Monotony, whatever causes it, robs writing of energy. Professional writers eliminate one cause of monotony by varying the length of their sentences. A succession of short sentences makes writing choppy, but a succession of long ones can make a reader drowsy.

Drawing again from one of the best, I offer as an example the following passage from the opening chapter of Zinsser's *On Writing Well:*

> Five or six years ago a school in Connecticut held "a day devoted to the arts," and I was asked if I would come and talk about writing as a vocation. When I arrived I found that a second speaker had been invited – Dr. Brock (as I'll call him), a surgeon who had recently begun to write and had sold some stories to national

magazines. He was going to talk about writing as an avocation. That made us a panel, and we sat down to face a crowd of student newspaper editors and reporters, English teachers and parents, all eager to learn the secrets of our glamorous work.

Dr. Brock was dressed in a bright red jacket, looking vaguely Bohemian, as authors are supposed to look, and the first question went to him. What was it like to be a writer?

He said it was tremendous fun. Coming home from an arduous day at the hospital, he would go straight to his yellow pad and write his tensions away. The words just flowed. It was easy.

I said that writing wasn't easy and it wasn't fun. It was hard and lonely, and the words seldom just flowed.

Read the passage slowly, and savor the pace of the writing as the anecdote unfolds. Picture the jovial Dr. Brock beside Zinsser, a former newspaperman who probably had *written* more words than the doctor had *read*, excepting, perhaps, the doctor's medical texts. I doubt that Zinsser *consciously* varied the length of his sentences; more likely, his talent, his experience, his ear for cadences guided him in the placement of periods.

MAKE EVERY WORD WORK HARD

A team, a committee, or a task force cannot do its best when some of its members are not carrying their weight. The same is true of writing. Business writing is replete with slovenly words that hang on like leeches, sucking the blood from the productive words. At the risk of mixing metaphors, I'll call them "weasel words." They hedge. They modify when no modification is needed. They rob the "team" of its energy. They are to writing what *you know* is to speaking.

Examples are seemingly innocuous words and phrases such as *very, quite, in other words, rather, pretty much, sort of,* and *in a very real sense.* You no doubt can add to the list. Most of the time they don't do any work, and they should be kicked off the team. Some of them, some of the time, do serve useful purposes — but not many and not often.

Make a list of weasel words. When one of them pops up in your writing, examine its function carefully. If you can do without it, pop it right out.

GIVE THOSE TIRED WORDS AND PHRASES A REST

Business writing has more than its share of tired, hackneyed words and phrases. Some of them once served honorably but should have been retired a hundred years ago. Others never should have been used at all. Still others are words of relatively recent vintage that became exhausted during a brief, but intense, time of use. They are the verbal equivalent of the Nehru jacket. A few have a bit of useful life remaining, if they are used sparingly.

Clichés are energy thieves. They also expose the writer as one who is either too lacking in imagination to find a fresh way to say something or too lazy to use the imagination he has.

EXERCISE 6: TIRED WORDS AND PHRASES

Here is a list of words and phrases common in business writing. Some of them are so old-fashioned that they have no place in modern prose. Others are simply overused. All have alternatives that are shorter and usually better. In the space beside each, supply an alternative.

in the event of _____ if _____

terminate _____

interface _____

early on _____

on a daily basis _____

at this time _____

close proximity to _____

a check in the amount of _____

first established _____

visible to the eye _____

exact same _____

a week's time _____

timeframe _____

honest truth _____

brown in color _____

relative to _____

thanking you in advance _____

each and every

first and foremost

one and only

refer back to

in the process of

the month of December

per your request

pursuant to

enclosed please find

remuneration

currently

forwarded

ascertain

feel free to call

thanking you I remain

utilize

interrogate

the undersigned

expedite

relate

communicate

above-mentioned

at your earliest convenience

for the purpose of

optimum

due to the fact that

EXERCISE 7: ADDING VIGOR

The passage below contains many of the faults discussed in the first three chapters — excess words, weak verbs, "dead" sentences, expletives, passive constructions, and tired words and phrases. Rewrite the passage to make it shorter and more vigorous.

We must first and foremost have discussions on the matter with property owners in the area, and then application will be made for a construction permit. A lot of factors will have to put into the hopper and taken into consideration before a final decision can be made on whether or not to proceed further.

If it turns out that it is necessary to make revisions in our site plan or to alter our plan of action in any way or fashion, studies will be undertaken by our engineering personnel to develop alternatives for presentation to property owners to make a determination as to which they have a preference for. If too many problems are experienced or encountered, the project can be abandoned in its entirety.

4.
How to Say
What You Mean

*When you have said something, make
sure you have said it. The chances of
your having said it are only fair.*
— William Strunk, Jr. and E. B. White,
The Elements of Style

Were Strunk and White, recognized authorities on writing, a couple of cynics? Having read the quotation above, you would be justified in saying so. But perhaps they were just being realistic. Perhaps they had read too many sentences like this one, which I heard on a radio commentary:

The governor is the penultimate politician.

Or this, from a metropolitan daily newspaper:

Psychologist B. F. Skinner . . . will discuss how behavioral analysis has influenced the use of the computer in the classroom at 11 a.m.

Or this, from a sales letter:

We understand that when an employee is not distracted from hunger or riding elevators to the buildings break area is a more productive employee.

Or this, from the sports page of a large daily:

Palmer, lacking his usual good fastball, pitched well for five innings.

Or this, from a letter written by the public relations manager of a multinational company:

We extend special respect to Mrs. _____ whose unique capabilities are truly ignobling.

Did the writers of those sentences say what they meant? If the governor is the next-to-last politician, who is the last? Did Dr. Skinner pinpoint the time that the behavioral analysis has influenced the use of the computer in the classroom? Can an employee be distracted from hunger? Did Palmer pitch well because he lacked his usual good fastball? And did Mrs. _____ know she had been insulted? Sad to say, examples like these are not hard to find. All but one are the work of professionals. Ignorance? Carelessness? The effect is the same in either case.

This chapter will discuss some things you should do — and some you should *not* do — if you want to be certain you have said what you wanted to say.

BRING BACK MISS GRUNDY

For many people, grammar is a turnoff. The word alone may be enough to strike fear in otherwise brave hearts. Perhaps it brings back memories of hours spent learning a lot of dreary rules under the stern direction of a teacher who seemed more concerned with the rules themselves than with the clear writing the rules were supposed to produce. Such teachers did exist, of course. They've been called "Miss Thistlebottom" and "Miss Grundy" — and probably some other names better left unmentioned.

But the Miss Grundys of the world weren't all bad. They understood something many modern teachers apparently do not: Learning grammatical principles and applying them is a form of discipline, and discipline is essential to writing. Perhaps it is true that Miss Grundy was more of a disciplinarian than an inspirer of young writers; but she knew how to craft a simple, declarative sentence. You can bet she always said exactly what she meant to say. Her devotion to the rules of grammar helped ensure clarity, order, and consistency. Many writers today could use a little of what Miss Grundy taught.

Some people write well with little or no knowledge of grammar, just as some musicians play the piano with little or no knowledge of music theory. But the best writers *and* the best musicians have the "ear" as well as knowledge gained from work and study.

This does not mean that you must undertake a study of grammar to improve your writing. It does mean that you should develop enough sensitivity to grammar to know when to turn to your grammar book and look up the rule. If you don't have a grammar book, get one and keep it at hand. Get a handbook, not a college or high school textbook. The one I use most is *The Handbook of Good English,* by Edward D. Johnson. Its explanations are clear and simple, and the book is organized for quick reference. It is neither permissive nor excessively restrictive in its approach to grammatical rules.

EXERCISE 8: GRAMMATICAL PRINCIPLES

The purpose of this exercise is to make you conscious of some important grammatical principles. In my discussion of the exercises in Appendix A, I'll explain the principles so that you can apply them in similar situations.

Each of the following sentences violates at least one principle of grammar. Read each one carefully. Identify the errors and decide on the best way to correct them. Chances are you'll be able to do this with many of the examples even though you may not recall the rules.

1. The president, whose term in office had barely begun when the opposition in Congress, which included many members of his own party, capitulated to public opinion, changing the nature of his party leadership. [From *The Handbook of Good English.*]

2. She writes as well or better than many professional writers.

3. He either will or already has mailed a check.

4. Like the manager, the employee's view of the problem was unrealistic.

5. He was fired from the job for sloppy work and drinking.

6. Billy has either gone fishing with his brother, or his father has taken him to the movies.

7. I like golfing, swimming, and to play chess.

8. He is a good employee, but I dislike him taking so long for lunch.

9. My dog didn't show up for his supper, and the next day I told my son it was missing.

10. Everyone must do their best to make the project successful.

11. Don't remove the cake from the box if you plan to give it to John.

12. The resources of the company were significant, but the ability of the owners to make the best use of them was reduced after they became tied up in litigation.

In the sentences below, choose the correct word or words from the alternative given.

1. The caller asked to speak with (whoever/whomever) was in charge of the project.

2. The ability to write well, we believe, is one of the many things that (set/sets) her apart.

3. She did not object to the (employees/employees') smoking in the restroom. In fact, she didn't mind (them/their) smoking in the office.

4. The company sent (he and I/him and me/him and I) to the seminar.

5. Address the letter to (whoever/whomever) it may concern.

6. I decided I would go if the boss (was/were) going to be there.

7. Her purse, with her checkbook and all her credit cards, (was/were) stolen.

8. The men or the girl (was/were) given the money.

9. The men, not the girl, (was/were) given the money.

10. The committee (is/are) qualified to judge the artist's work.

11. Physics (is/are) among the most difficult subjects I have studied.

12. The United States, and most western nations, (embraces/embrace) free enterprise.

13. The United States and most western nations (embrace/embraces) free enterprise.

14. If I (were/was) you, I would write a letter to protest the poor service.

15. I felt (bad/badly) about making the error.

16. "Do not go (gentle/gently) into that good night."

17. He plays golf much better than (me/I).

18. That's (he/him) — the man (who/whom) you identified at the trial.

19. The data (is/are) not yet available.

20. Having coffee and doughnuts in the office each morning (is/are) something we look forward to.

PUNCTUATE FOR CLARITY

Punctuation marks are to reading as traffic signs and signals are to driving. They tell the reader when to slow down, when to stop, and what's ahead. They also define the relationship of one sentence element to another. When traffic signals are clear and well placed, driving is easier. When punctuation marks are used properly, reading is easier. The writer who wants to have his work read and understood will use punctuation with skill and care.

Punctuation has few unbreakable rules. Punctuation styles and preferences vary considerably even among the best writers. The modern way is to use as little punctuation, especially commas, as possible. Carried to extreme, this can result in ambiguity. Over-punctuating, on the other hand, can make writing ponderous. The conscientious writer takes punctuation seriously, adhering generally to accepted conventions while applying the criteria of clarity and meaning.

To understand how punctuation can affect meaning, read the two sentences below and let your ear tell you how they differ:

Our Florida plant, located near Miami, employs more than 250 people.

Our Florida plant located near Miami employs more than 250 people.

In the first sentence, the words *located near Miami* are set off by commas. They simply describe the plant. They add to the information the reader is given, but they *are not* essential to the meaning. In the second sentence, the same words without the commas *are* essential because they tell the reader *which* Florida plant employs more than 250 people. The first sentence clearly implies that the company has only one plant in Florida, and it is located near Miami. The second implies that the company has more than one Florida plant, and the one the writer is referring to is located near Miami.

The meaning of each of those sentences depends upon two little commas. Putting commas where they are not needed and omitting them where they are needed are among the most common errors in punctuation.

The following sentences provide another interesting illustration of how a comma affects meaning:

> She did not accept the transfer because she wanted to earn more money.

> She did not accept the transfer, because she wanted to earn more money.

The first sentence means that she accepted the transfer, but she did so for a reason other than the money. The second says that she did not accept the transfer, and it implies that the reason she did not accept it was that it would not have paid her more money.

Ordinarily, a dependent clause such as *because she wanted more money* would not be preceded by a comma. When a *because* clause follows a negative statement, however, a comma may be needed. A thoughtful writer will consider carefully whether a comma is needed to express the desired meaning.

Court cases have been decided by punctuation. According to one anecdote, a comma inserted into federal statute where no comma had been might have altered the course of history. The story is told somewhat drily in the *American Journal of International Law,* October 1940, in an article titled "The Attorney General's Opinion on the Exchange of Destroyers for Naval Bases." Here is a summary:

Shortly before America's entry into World War II, Great Britain was in dire straits. The Germans were bombing London almost daily. President Franklin D. Roosevelt wanted to aid the Britons by sending them war material, and he sought a way to do so despite strong pacifist sentiment against it. Roosevelt concocted a plan by which the United States would provide destroyers to Britain and Britain would allow U.S. Naval vessels to be based there. The President asked his attorney general, Robert Jackson, for an opinion on whether the plan was legal.

Johnson determined that the pertinent federal statute was the Neutrality Act of 1917. As written, that law seemed to prohibit the President's proposed plan. But Jackson, presumably, shared Roosevelt's sentiments about helping Britain in her darkest hour. He inserted a comma into a key sentence of the act, changing the meaning of the law — or at least making it ambiguous enough so that Roosevelt chose to interpret it his way. As far as I know, it was never tested in court, probably because Japanese bombs on December 7, 1941, eliminated opposition to helping our allies.

Although the comma is the most frequently used punctuation, the period is the most *under*used. In much business writing, clarity could be increased by the simple device of breaking long sentences into shorter ones.

In Chapter 9 we'll discuss punctuation in greater detail.

CHOOSE THE RIGHT WORD

Mark Twain wrote, "The difference between the right word and the almost right word is the difference between lightning and lightning bug."

Good writing does not require an enormous vocabulary, but it does require that the writer choose his words well. This means choosing the right word to convey the intended meaning. It means never using a word unless you're certain what it means. It means being aware of the precise meaning, not just the definition found in the dictionary. It means understanding the emotional impact of words.

Words can create a perception that is more important than reality. For example, I read of a survey in which a majority of respondents said they were against "social welfare." In another survey, taken at the same time and using a similar sample of the population, respondents said they favored "aid to poor people." That's understandable: *Social welfare* evokes the old "welfare Cadillac" vision, but few Americans lack compassion for the poor.

Another interesting example comes from the debate, in 1987

and 1988, over military support of the Nicarauguan Contras. Opponents adopted the slogan, "Give peace a chance" — a strong emotional appeal. Proponents had nothing similar. Someone suggested that if the proponents had used "Give freedom a chance" as their rallying cry, their message might have swayed more people to their point of view.

Three basic tools can help you use words more effectively. The first is a standard dictionary. A dictionary attempts to give all possible meanings of a word, but it is not always a reliable guide to correct usage. Some of the newer dictionaries include thousands of words that have come into the language in recent years. They are excellent.

In addition to a standard dictionary, every writer should have a usage manual. Many are available. The one I use most often is the *Harper Dictionary of Contemporary Usage*, by William and Mary Morris. If you want to know, for example, when to use *on behalf of* rather than *in behalf of*, you can find the answer there. Or if you'd like to know whether *importantly* or *important* is preferred in **Most important(ly)**, William and Mary have the answer. The judgments are not the Morrises' alone. They were arrived at in consultation with a panel consisting of writers and other respected professionals. They are not so much prescriptive as descriptive: They describe how the language is used by reasonably well-educated people, which means the book is neither pedantic nor excessively permissive. Comments of panel members are included with many entries, and they are worth reading.

A third tool that will help you use words more effectively is a dictionary of synonyms. I have a copy of Hayakawa's *Modern Guide to Synonyms and Related Words*. This is *not* a thesaurus. A thesaurus will give many synonyms from which you can choose one that might say what you want to say. Hayawaka's *Guide* is more discriminating in the synonyms it suggests, and it gives different connotations for each so that you can pick the best one. The entry for *misery*, for example, lists *agony, anguish, distress, passion,* and *torture.* In the discussion of connotations, we're informed that *misery* refers to "a chronic or prolonged suffering, whether physical, mental, or emotional." Compare that with *agony*, which "represents suffering the endurance of which calls forth every human resource." This book is worth owning.

I am often asked whether a thesaurus is worth owning. The answer is, probably yes; but I confess that I seldom use mine.

Chapter 8, "Know the Difference," is a quick-reference guide to some troublesome words and phrases.

EXERCISE 9: WORD USAGE

Each of the sentences below contains one or more words used incorrectly. Try to pick them out. Unless you're exceptional, you'll have some surprises.

1. When the police arrived, the body was ~~laying~~ *lying* on the ground ~~in a prone position~~, staring at the sky with lifeless eyes.

2. The football team was weak on defense, but ~~it's~~ *its* offense was ~~bombastic.~~ *strong*

3. We will ~~disperse~~ *disburse* the funds by January 30.

4. The heroin of the story was a teenage model.

5. The basic ~~criteria~~ *criterion* of good writing is clearity.

6. The lessee customarily pays the rent in advance, but the mortgagee makes his house payment in arrears.

7. Media advertising campaigns and sales promotions are most effective when they are ~~carried~~ out in ~~tandem.~~ *or* *concurrently*

8. Six pretty cheerleaders, waving pom-poms, ~~flouted~~ their youthful exuberance in front of 50,000 fans. *flaunted*

9. Mr. Jones's tie complimented his suit.

10. The company's earnings decreased 200 percent this year.

11. Noisome children are especially distracting to older people.

12. This book is three times as thin as the other.

13. The high school principle was a man of high principals, and he would never sacrifice those principles to add to his principal.

14. In his speech, the President ~~inferred~~ that the leak came from someone in the Senate. *suggested* *implied*

15. The best policy is to prevent the problem before it occurs.

THE LANGUAGE OF CONTROL

To *control* the meaning of what you write, use specific, concrete words rather than generalities or abstractions. The use of abstract words allows the reader, not the writer, to control the meaning. For example, a sentence like **Several members were absent from the meeting** lets the reader decide how many were absent; but if you write **Five members were absent,** you give the reader no choice. You, the writer, retain control of the meaning. Specific, concrete words are the language of control.

Is *machine* a concrete word, or is it an abstract word? Ask that of a group, and chances are about half will answer one way and half the other. Both answers are right. And both are wrong.

A concrete word is *exclusive*. An abstract word is *inclusive*. The most inclusive word I can think of at the moment is *thing*. It excludes nothing. The most exclusive word I can think of is *me* because it excludes everything and everybody but me.

Machine excludes everything that isn't a machine, but it includes cotton gins, looms, bicycles, dentists' drills, typewriters, food processors, air compressors, automobiles, and aircraft.

Aircraft is more exclusive than *machine,* but it includes blimps, helicopters, biplanes, and jets.

A jet can be a fighter, a bomber, or an airliner.

An airliner can be an L1011, a DC-9, or a 747.

And a 747? Isn't that about as specific as you can get? Not exactly. You can specify a Delta 747, and old 747, a white 747, or the 747 that at this very moment is landing at O'Hare International Airport.

The point is, the more concrete the word — you can call it exclusive or specific if you prefer — the more precise its meaning. Good writing does not require that only concrete words be used. The writer must decide whether his purpose is served with generalities or whether the purpose requires the precision that only the language of control can provide.

EXERCISE 10: THE LANGUAGE OF CONTROL

I call this exercise "The Incredible Unflunkable Reading Test." It's not only unflunkable, it's also unpassable. That's because it has no correct answers. Try it anyway. Read the narrative and then take your best shot at answering the questions. Look back at the narrative all you like. The only rule is that you must give actual numbers and other specific information for your answers, not generalities such as *a lot.*

Senator Pfillmore Pfogbottom is a veteran of the U.S. Senate. In 1980 he was reelected by an overwhelming majority. He's not a wealthy man, but before his election to the Senate he earned a comfortable living as a lawyer. His wife, Pfanny Pfae Pfogbottom, is executive director of the Beltway Voyeur Society and commands a salary in the five-figure range.

The Senator is known throughout official Washington as an unparalleled raconteur on the Senate floor and an enthusiastic roué in his off-duty time. He also plays golf, but he can't make it to the Burning Tree Country Club very often, due to the press of business. He is considered a very good golfer for one who plays so seldom.

Senator and Mrs. Pfogbottom have two children, Pfineas, who is 17, and Pfyllis, 14. Pfineas plays basketball on his high school team, and the coach describes him as "a scrappy player and a valuable member of the team in spite of the fact that he is of only average height." Pfyllis loves to read and usually reads several books a month. She is, however, addicted to "trashy" books. Her parents admit she isn't a "brain," but they insist she is a good student. The only other member of the household is Mrs. Pfogbottom's old-maid aunt.

The Senator is best known for having introduced a bill related to the exportation of microwave ovens to Ethiopia. It was defeated decisively.

Now that you know the Pfogbottom saga, pfill in the blanks below:

1. How long has Pfogbottom been a Senator? _____

2. What percentage of the vote did he receive in the election of 1980? _____

3. What is his net worth? _____

4. How much did he earn annually as a lawyer? _____

5. What is Pfanny Pfae's salary? _____

6. What is a typical golf score for Pfogbottom? _____

7. Where does he play? _____

8. How often does he play? _____

9. How tall is Pfineas? _____

10. How many books does Pfyllis read in a typical month? ___

11. What is her grade average? _____

12. How old is Mrs. Pfogbottom's aunt? _____

13. Was Senator Pfogbottom's bill for or against exporting microwave ovens to Ethiopia? _____

14. How many senators voted against the bill? _____

I'm sure you get the idea. The purpose of this is to have a bit of fun and to dramatize the impossibility of communicating precisely without using concrete language. In my seminars, answers to the questions vary all over. Some participants say Pfanny Pfae's "five figure" salary is $10,000; others say $99,000. To some, an "overwhelming majority" in an election is 90 percent; to others, anything more than 50 percent is overwhelming because it "overwhelms" the opponent.

Ask several friends to take the Incredible Unflunkable Reading Test. You'll enjoy seeing how they react.

THE WAGES OF SYNTAX

Whenever I mention *syntax* to a group, some wiseacre invariably says something like, "Well, if we gotta have a tax, I suppose a sin tax is the best kind to have."

That's old, but it still is good for a laugh. Once the laughter stops, I explain that syntax refers to the arrangement of sentence elements in their proper relationship to each other. Without intending to get bogged down in definitions, let me say that I'm broadening the idea of syntax just a bit for this discussion.

Bad syntax prevents the writer from saying what is meant, and it often leaves the reader confused. As Follett wrote, "Prose is not necessarily good because it obeys the rules of syntax, but it is fairly certain to be bad if it ignores them."

Within my broadened definition I have identified five forms of bad syntax — danglers, non sequiturs, misplaced modifiers, unclear antecedents, and lack of parallelism. You can avoid most of them by thinking carefully about what you have written, rather than just putting words together. Good syntax is a product of clear thinking. As the old song says, you can't have one without the other.

Danglers. A dangler is a clause or a phrase that is placed near something it cannot logically relate to. Danglers are sometimes called *dangling participles* because most often a participial phrase is what dangles. For example, **Standing more than six and a half feet tall, I assumed the man was the basketball player** flouts logic. It *says* that *I* stand more than six and a half feet tall. It *means* that I see a man who stands six and a half feet tall and who I assume is the basketball player.

Examples like that are obvious and usually are the work of careless writers, but even good writers occasionally slip on something like **Known as Mister October, Reggie Jackson's record in World Series play is inspiring to young ball players.** Of course, it's Reggie Jackson who is known as Mister October, not his record.

Non sequiturs. Non sequitur is a Latin term loosely translated as *it does not follow.* A non sequitur is an irrelevancy that results from a writer's putting a piece of information where it doesn't belong. The most common examples are in such constructions as **Born in Alabama, Joe Louis became one of the greatest boxers of all time.** Unless the writer has demonstrated some relationship between Louis's having been born in Alabama and his having become a great boxer, the two thoughts don't belong together. **Born in Alabama, Joe Louis became known worldwide as one of the greatest boxers of all time** is logical because the writer clearly is contrasting Louis's Alabama origin with his worldwide celebrity.

Born in Scotland, MacDuff opened his first store at the age of twenty-five is a non sequitur. **Born in Scotland, Mr. Mac-Duff has played the bagpipes since he was six** is logical because of the natural association of bagpipes with Scotsmen.

Non sequiturs also occur in the middle of sentences, although mid-sentence non sequiturs don't seem nearly as bad as those that begin sentences.

Theodore Bernstein, the late assistant managing editor of *The New York Times* and author of several books on usage, had this to say about non sequiturs:

If two pieces of information are to be linked in physical proximity, they should also be linked in meaning. . . . If a couple of facts are in no way tied together, they should be as separate in writing as they are in life. [From *The Careful Writer.*]

Misplaced modifiers. Generally, modifiers — adjectives, adverbs, and adverbial and adjectival clauses — should be placed as near as possible to whatever they modify. When this is not done, the result can be sentences that fail to say what the writer intended. Following are some examples that illustrate this principle:

TV's insatiable appetite for fresh grief eats up sobbing fire, flood or crime victims. . . . [From *The Wall Street Journal.*]

Southland Corp., the parent company of 7-Eleven Stores . . . announced it would no longer sell any men's magazines in April. [*The Atlanta Journal*]

While the ambulance was being last Tuesday used to transport the voter, Lillian Hughes became ill and collapsed. [Associated Press]

[Senator Sam] Nunn said earlier this year that he would decide whether to form an exploratory committee — the first official step in a presidential campaign — by the end of this month. [*The Atlanta Constitution*]

In the first example the misplaced modifier is *sobbing,* which belongs next to *victims,* not *fire.* Fires have been known to roar, crackle, rage, and tower, but never, to my knowledge, has a fire sobbed. The sentence illustrates not only the misplacement of a modifier but also the pitfalls of thoughtlessly converting nouns to adjectives, as we discussed in Chapter 2. The only way in which the writer could have put *sobbing* in its proper place was to use *fire, flood,* and *crime* as nouns rather than twisting them into adjectives. Thus, we would have ". . . sobbing victims of fire, flood, or crime. . . ."

In the second example, *in April* is when Southland Corp. made its momentous announcement. Taking the sentence literally, a reader would assume that he would have to wait until May to pick up his copy of *Playboy* at a 7-Eleven store.

For awkwardness of expression, the third example wins the pole position. I can only surmise that the AP staffer who wrote *last Tuesday used* was "spooked" by the journalistic prejudice against chronological order. The natural way to tell what happened to the unfortunate Ms. Hughes would be *Last Tuesday, while the ambulance was being used to transport the voter . . ..* An acceptable alternative would be *While the ambulance was being used last Tuesday to transport the voter . . ..* Miss Grundy probably would have chastised the writer of the original version for separating the main verb, *used,* from its auxiliary, *was being,* by inserting *last Tuesday* between them.

The reporter who wrote the sentence in the fourth example probably knew that what Senator Nunn said was that he would decide "by the end of this month" whether to form an exploratory committee. A reader might infer, especially on hurried reading, that the Senator could form the committee by the end of the month. I have been accused of nitpicking for my criticism of that sentence. If that's nitpicking, I accept it and consider it a badge of honor. To write well, you have to be a nitpicker. Besides, even the slightest possibility of ambiguity could have been eliminated by putting *by the end of this month* immediately after *decide,* where it belongs.

The word *only* is especially bothersome to many writers. Moving it around in a sentence results in subtle changes in meaning. The five sentences below differ only in the position of *only.* See whether you agree that the meaning of each is slightly different.

John vowed only to date Mary. (This could mean that to date Mary was the only vow John made.)

John vowed to only date Mary. (This could imply that John vowed to date Mary, but not to marry her.)

John only vowed to date Mary. (Two meanings are possible: John was the only person who vowed to date Mary, or John vowed to date Mary, but that's all he did.)

John vowed to date only Mary. (This is unambiguous.)

John vowed to date Mary only. (This means the same as the previous sentence except that it is more emphatic. The end of a sentence has the greatest impact on the reader.)

Adjectives usually precede the words they modify, but good usage requires that adverbs be placed *after* the verbs in most cases. **The bride slowly walked down the aisle** is not incorrect, but **The bride walked slowly down the aisle** is much the better word order. It is also the natural word order; it's the order you probably would use in speaking. Skillful writers know when they can safely depart from natural word order. You may have noticed that the adverbs *usually* in the first sentence of this paragraph and *probably* in the second come before their verbs. That's because *precede usually* and *would use probably* are awkward.

In The **President of the United States sat behind the desk,** the phrase *behind the desk,* which modifies *sat,* is in its proper position. Turned around to read **Behind the desk sat the President of the United States,** the sentence is more dramatic and interesting.

Unclear Antecedents. In grammar, an antecedent is a word that comes before, and defines, a pronoun. In **I read the book and liked it,** *book* is the antecedent of *it.* The important things to know about antecedents are (1) a pronoun and its antecedent must be of the same person, number, and gender, and (2) the antecedent must be clear to the reader; otherwise the sentence might be ambiguous. Unclear — or nonexistent — antecedents are a common problem. A little understanding and a lot of clear thinking can solve it.

A classic example of ambiguity resulting from an unclear antecedent is **John asked Bill whether he could play second base.** The reader can only guess whether the antecedent of *he* is *John* or *Bill.* The sentence could mean either John asked Bill for permission to play second base or John asked Bill whether he (Bill) was capable of playing second base, depending on which of the two possible antecedents the reader assigned to *he.*

Sentences such as **If your kitten won't drink cold milk, put it in the microwave oven for a few seconds** make the writer seem foolish.

Unclear antecedents in legal documents can pose serious problems. Writing consultant V. C. (Vee) Nelson, who specializes in helping attorneys write better, warns against ambiguity resulting from unclear antecedents. Dr. Nelson cites a legal maxim, the doctrine of last antecedent, that states, essentially, that when the meaning of a legal document is in doubt because of an unclear antecedent, the last antecedent controls the interpretation. If the originator of the document had something else in mind, well, that's too bad.

Other authorities on legal language have warned attorneys that bad writing could get them into trouble.

Although an antecedent is, by definition, a word or words that *precede* the pronoun, some writers try to vary their sentence structure by putting the pronoun *before* its antecedent. Example: **You might not believe it, but the lesson in the second chapter is the most important thing you'll learn about the subject.** What does *it* refer to? Has the writer said that you might not believe the lesson, or that you might not believe the lesson is the most important thing you'll learn about the subject? Putting the antecedent after, rather than before, makes ambiguity all the more likely. It also seems vaguely unfriendly to the reader because it delays his understanding of the message. Be cautious about putting the antecedent ahead of its pronoun. Follett devotes almost six pages in *Modern American Usage* to antecedents. Those pages are worth a read.

Parallelism. Parallelism means that sentence elements should be parallel in grammatical form if they are parallel in meaning. This is not an easy concept to get across, but it is worth knowing about. Attention to parallelism can help ensure clear, stylish writing.

To take a simple example, consider this sentence, which you will recall from Exercise 8: **I like golfing, swimming, and to play chess.** The lack of parallelism in that sentence is roughly equivalent to a bass fiddle in the violin section. Your ear tells you immediately that it should be **I like golfing, swimming, and playing chess** or, simply, **I like golf, swimming, and chess.** The reason your ear finds the first version so offensive is that *golfing, swimming,* and *to play* are not parallel in grammatical construction. *Golfing* and *swimming* are gerunds; *to play* is an infinitive. The other two versions are gentle to the ear because the parallelism, although not exact, is within acceptable limits.

In another sentence from Exercise 8, we have a more subtle example of faulty parallelism:

> Billy has either gone fishing with his brother, or his father has taken him to the movies.

Either . . . or is a pair of correlatives, so called because they establish a relationship between elements that have similar functions and should be grammatically parallel. The sentence above has two predicates, has *gone* and has *taken,* each with its own subject. The position of *either* seems to indicated that the two predicates share a subject, which is not the case. To correct the faulty parallelism, change the location of *either*. Thus, in **Either Billy has gone fishing with his brother, or his father has taken him to the movies,** the sentence element relating to *either* is grammatically parallel to the sentence element relating to *or*. **Billy has gone either fishing with his brother or to the movies with his father** also is correct even though *fishing* and to the *movies* are not, strictly speaking, parallel. Here common sense must prevail: There is no good way to make *fishing* and to the *movies* exactly parallel, since you could not say Billy has gone "movieing." Both elements — the first a participle, the second a prepositional phrase — function as adverbs modifying has *gone*. *Fishing*, in this example, describes a destination rather than an activity.

I like to think of *either . . . or, not only . . . but also,* and other correlatives as being like old-fashioned balance scales. The "weight" of whatever is on one side must equal that of whatever is on the other in order for the scale to be in balance.

When items are listed in a series, they must be of the same part of speech in order to parallel — nouns with nouns, verbs with verbs, and so on. **Mary is intelligent, talented, attractive, and plays a good game of golf** is an example of faulty parallelism in a series. It should read **Mary is intelligent, talented, and attractive, and she plays a good game of golf.** In sentences like that, having two *ands* bothers some writers. It shouldn't.

A series in which the first item is introduced by an article (*a, an, the*) should use the article either with the first word only or with all words in the series. For example, **The man ordered a steak, salad, and a dessert** is unacceptable. It could read either **The man ordered a steak, salad, and dessert** or **The man ordered a steak, a salad, and a dessert.** The latter is preferable. In a sentence such as **The company has hired a public relations firm, advertising agency, accounting firm, and law firm,** use of the article with each item in the series is mandated by the fact that *a* cannot serve both *public relations firm* and *advertising agency*. The sentence must be changed to **The company has hired *a* public relations firm, *an* advertising agency, *an* accounting firm, and *a* law firm.**

The same principle applies to prepositional phrases in series. If all the phrases call for the same preposition, you need not repeat it after the first use. If you choose to use the preposition with any of the other phrases, you must use it with all of them.

This afternoon I went to the supermarket, the barber shop, the hardware store, and to the service station violates this principle. Either insert *to* before *the barber shop* and *the hardware store* or remove it from in front of *service station*.

In the following sentence, faulty parallelism results in ambiguity:

> The chairman told the shareholders that sales volume dropped sharply during the fourth quarter, that revenue would be less than in the previous year, and the price of the company's stock has declined by twenty percent.

The reader does not know whether the chairman told the shareholders that the price of the company's stock declined by twenty percent as a result of the decline in revenue, or whether the stock price declined by twenty percent as a result of the chairman's statement to the shareholders. If the writer meant the latter, placement of *that* after *and* in the last clause was necessary to make the meaning clear.

Many writers, including some professionals, neglect parallelism. When they do, they put clarity as well as style at risk.

DON'T OVERSTUFF YOUR SENTENCES

This is not an admonition to refrain from writing long sentences. A skillful writer can write a long sentence that is not only comprehensible but also graceful. But when a writer tries to pack too much information into a sentence, especially when the bits of information are not closely related, both comprehension and grace are likely to be sacrificed. Consider the following examples quoted by James J. Kilpatrick in a syndicated newspaper column:

> "Silent Cal has gotten a raw deal," says Rep. Silvio Conti, a Massachusetts Republican who persuaded the House to declare last week the first annual Calvin Coolidge Week, marking the 60th anniversary of his swearing-in after Warren G. Harding's death by his notary public father in the family home in Plymouth Notch, Vt. [*Newsweek*]

> TEL AVIV — The 16-1 vote followed a grenade explosion in a crowd of Peace Now demonstrators outside a cabinet meeting that killed a paratrooper who friends said fought in the Lebanon invasion

and injured nine others who demanded Sharon be fired. [United Press International]

Founded in 1843 — and edited later in the century by Walter Bagehot, the period's most famous English journalist of democratic politics and capitalist economics — the weekly's circulation has doubled to about 200,000 over the past decade. [*The Washington Post*]

Let's analyze the first sentence. Never mind what we think it is *supposed* to mean. What it *says* is (1) Last week marked the 60th anniversary of Rep. Conti's swearing-in, and (2) Warren Harding was killed by his own father.

Consider the second sentence: Did the cabinet meeting kill a paratrooper? Did the paratrooper injure nine "others"?

The third sentence says the weekly's circulation was founded in 1843 and edited by Walter Bagehot.

Those three sentences cited by Mr. Kilpatrick as examples of "sentence packing" came from major news media. So that you won't suppose me to be prejudiced, I offer two examples from the public relations profession:

Paul Ridings Public Relations, Inc. — which became the first public relations firm in the Southwest to own its own building in 1956 when it bought the building at 3467 West Freeway where it had been a tenant for the year previous, starting July 1, 1955, when the firm was founded — has moved. [The lead sentence of a news release]

That could be the only time the history of a public relations firm was written in a single sentence. And I only hope that the following is not typical of the writing done by the PR firm that produced it:

The trend in society toward a dissolution of divisions between the public and private sectors, toward a multi-institutional, knowledge-based global economy, and the increasing role that corporations are playing in employee training, development and education, and the pervasive need to communicate the constant, rapid social and economic changes that characterize the Information Age, are among the current pressures shaping the future of communications management. [From a document titled "Public Relations Research and Organizational Change"]

In 1958, in his book *Watch Your Language,* Theodore Bernstein advanced the notion that sentences might be limited to one idea each as a means of ensuring clarity and instant comprehension. The notion was based on research that showed writing with one-idea sentences was significantly easier to comprehend than writing with compound sentences having two or more ideas each. The proposition is difficult to disagree with.

Rewriting the first of the sentences from the Kilpatrick column to break it into several one-idea sentences, I came up with this:

> "Silent Cal has gotten a raw deal, says Rep. Silvio Conti. The Massachusetts Republican persuaded the House to declare last week the first annual Calvin Coolidge to mark the 60th anniversary of Coolidge's swearing-in. Coolidge succeeded to the presidency after the death of Warren G. Harding. He was sworn-in by his father, a notary public, at the family home in Plymouth Notch, Vt.

I have written elsewhere with more style and grace, but I have never written more clearly.

Bernstein did not advocate adhering strictly to the one-idea-per-sentence concept. Nor do I. Still, it's worth considering, especially if your tendency is to overstuff sentences.

JARGON: HANDLE WITH CARE

Jargon is language peculiar to a particular profession or industry. Although jargon is often derided, it is useful as a sort of shorthand. It saves words and therefore makes communication more efficient. Consider, for example, the term *interface,* which is commonly used and readily understood by people who work with computers. When computer systems are compatible, they are said to *interface* with each other. I can't think of a better way to say it. The word does not pollute the language. It is not offensive to the ear.

The problem with *interface* is that it has spilled over into general usage, and in general usage there is no consensus about its meaning. I have asked fifty or sixty people to define the word in its nontechnical sense. The variety of answers I have received convinces me that it means something different to almost everyone.

In the jargon of the beverage industry, *sample* is used as a verb meaning to give away samples of a product. Thus, a soft-drink bottler might *sample* shoppers in a supermarket; but a shopper who was *sampled* would tell you that *he* sampled the product, meaning he tasted it. Clearly, the meaning of the word is different in industry jargon than in general usage.

One summer The Coca-Cola Company asked its bottlers to sponsor clinics for aspiring high school cheerleaders. A young man whose job was to help sell the idea to bottlers, wrote the following opening sentence for a promotional brochure: "Bottlers will have an opportunity to sample impressionable young girls this summer."

Using jargon indiscriminately is a lazy way to write. My advice is to keep jargon in its place. Never use it where there is even the slightest possibility that it will mean different things to different readers.

USE TRANSITIONS TO SIGNAL THE READER

One way to make your writing reader-friendly is to help the reader along by giving him an idea of what's ahead. Good punctuation and good sentence structure are two ways to accomplish this. Use of transitions is another.

A transition is a word, a phrase, or a sentence that tells a reader to expect a change of subject, a continuation, an example, or a modification of a previous statement. By telling the reader what's ahead, it prepares him to assimilate the information and in that way makes reading easier. The first sentence of a paragraph can be an effective transition if it eases the reader from one subject to another.

As an example of the effect of a transition, consider the following sentences:

> The company lost money in the fourth quarter. Profit for the year increased.

> The company lost money in the fourth quarter. Nevertheless, profit for the year increased.

The only difference between the two pairs of sentences is the addition of *nevertheless* in the second sentence of the second pair. But there is a great difference in how the reader would react.

Nevertheless is a transition that foretells a softening of the bad news contained in the first sentence.

The following is from a newspaper story about the discovery of new superconducting materials:

> Independent scientists also are enthusiastic [about the discovery]. They say the density of the electrical current passed by the new superconducting materials may be too low for some applications. And they say that the materials themselves, exotic metal oxides, are too brittle to be shaped into conventional electrical wiring.

The writer of that paragraph committed an unfriendly act against his readers. The first sentence of the paragraph — the topic sentence, if you prefer — signals the reader that the paragraph is going to say some positive things about the new materials. The signal, however, is false: The sentences that follow are negative. The writer could have used a transition such as *however, nevertheless,* or *even so* at the beginning of the second sentence. A better solution would have been to make the opening sentence something like this: **Most independent scientists also are enthusiastic, but some have expressed reservations about the discovery.**

The following words and phrases often function as transitions: *for example, in addition, however, first, nevertheless, as a result, consequently, to illustrate, finally, at the same time, also, but, to summarize, on the other hand, previously, furthermore, in conclusion, in other words.* Many of these transitions are overused, and your writing might be fresher if you find some alternatives to the most common ones.

Skillfully placed, transitions contribute to clarity and meaning. Overused, they can make writing tiresome. Your ear and your sense of logic should tell you when a transition is needed.

THINK, THINK, THINK

Most of the suggestions I have make in this chapter can be summarized in one word: *think.* To be certain you say what you mean, think about punctuation and grammar, about the words you choose, about how the words are arranged in the sentences, about how transitions can make your sentences "superconductors" of meaning.

I once told a colleague who asked me to criticize his writing that I thought his writing was okay but his thinking was lousy. He was shocked to hear me say that, for he was a bright young man with the academic credentials to prove it. But when I showed him examples of how he had failed to say what he meant, he began to understand the relationship of thinking to writing. Later he told me that his writing had greatly improved as a result of our conversation.

The problem is not confined to inexperienced writers. Sometimes a professional knows his subject so well that he forgets that the reader might not know the subject at all. An Associated Press article from July 1986 illustrates this point. The story was filed from New Orleans, Louisiana, site of the annual convention of Lions Club International. It concerned a proposal to change the Lions' by-laws to permit the induction of women. Its first two paragraphs were misleading:

> NEW ORLEANS — Lions Clubs International, which claims to be the world's largest service organization with more than 1.3 million members, voted Saturday against letting women join the club.
>
> With more than 6,600 votes counted of 7,500 cast, the proposed amendment failed by a margin of 59 percent to 41 percent, short of the two thirds majority required to change the Lions constitution.

The question is, how many members voted for the amendment and how many voted against it. "Failed by a margin of 59 percent to 41 percent" seems to say that 59 percent of the members were against and 41 percent were for. That, however, was not the case. The vote was 59 percent to 41 percent in *favor* of the amendment. The amendment failed because the favorable vote, although a majority, was not the two-thirds majority required to amend. The writer knew what he meant, but a casual reader almost certainly would have thought that a majority of the Lions were against admitting women.

Another example is from a story filed by Reuters news service of Great Britain:

> BERLIN — Western diplomats crossed into West Berlin on Tuesday in defiance of a new East German demand to show passports — a move that could be construed as recognition of the frontier as an international border.

Which move could be construed as recognition of the frontier as an international border — the diplomats' crossing into West Berlin, or the East Germans' demanding that passports be shown? The sentence suggests one answer, logic suggests another. The question was not resolved until four paragraphs later.

As a writer, you must not ask your readers to do your thinking for you. Your job is to get your message across as clearly as possible.

Writing and thinking are inseparable: You cannot write well if you cannot think clearly. And to an extent the converse is true: As you improve your writing you will increase your ability to think logically. That's an added bonus for working hard on your writing.

5.
Target the Writing to the Reader

The first and most important step in writing
is to know who you're writing to —
who they are and what they want.
—David G. Lyon, *The XYZ's of Business Writing*

"Have I reached the party to whom I am speaking?" goes a line from an old joke. But it's no joke when a writer asks himself whether he has reached the "party" to whom he is writing. It's a question every writer ought to ask before he signs off on a piece of copy. If he can't be certain he has reached his intended reader, then he can't be certain his efforts have not been wasted. An engineer who uses technical language in writing for nontechnical readers almost certainly wastes not only his time but his readers' time as well; yet engineers often do. So do lawyers, accountants, physicians, and others in specialized professions.

Would you write a business letter to someone you didn't know and use the same informal tone you would use in a letter to a close friend or relative? Of course not; yet some people do.

Language, tone, and style are essential parts of writing. They can determine how well the writing is targeted to its intended readers. In this chapter we'll discuss these and other ways in which you can be certain you have reached your "party."

INFORMALITY: HOW MUCH IS TOO MUCH?

Several years ago I received a letter from a recent college graduate who was interested in being interviewed for a job with the public relations firm where I am senior vice president. The letter was neatly typed and well-written. The résumé that accompanied it was impressive. I tossed it all into my wastebasket. I never even *thought* of responding. Why? Because the letter began with "Dear Richard."

Now, I have many young friends who call me by my given name. I'm not bothered by that. I encourage it. But I had never met this man. From his résumé I learned that he was younger than my own children. His poor judgment in addressing me, a stranger, by my first name led me to decide summarily that he did not belong in our firm. Had I been more disposed to kindness, I would have answered his letter if only to advise him to use better judgment in writing letters of application. In attempting to target his letter to me by using what he presumably thought was a friendly, informal salutation, he failed to "reach" me. His familiarity was simply out of place. He wasted his time.

We live in an age of informality, and the customs of the day are in many respects preferable to those of earlier, more formal times. Still, a writer must not assume that informality is always appropriate. This is a decision you must make when you write: Should the style be formal, informal, or something in between?

In planning this book I decided that a relaxed, relatively informal style would be appropriate for the men and women who would be most likely to buy the book. I wanted readers to *enjoy* the book, not to feel intimidated by it. The techniques through which I have tried to achieve that end include liberal use of contractions, personal pronouns, anecdotes from my experience as a writer, and some humor. In reading over my first draft I found that I had been almost flippant at times. I concluded that I had gone too far, and I made many changes to correct the problem in later drafts.

No one can decide for you how much informality is appropriate for a given piece of writing or a given audience. No rules exist except the "rule" of common sense. You must train yourself to think carefully about who your readers are and what they want — and about how you want them to react to your message.

SEEK A COMMON GROUND

The president of a large corporation kept prominently displayed in his office a photograph of an attractive family group — an elderly man and woman, a couple of bright-looking teenagers, and a woman, apparently near the executive's age, holding a baby. Visitors to the office often remarked on the picture, complimenting the man on his "fine family." Most of the time the executive merely smiled and thanked his visitor. Once, however, a visitor pursued the subject by asking whether the elderly man and woman were the executive's parents.

"No," the president replied. "In fact, I don't know who they are." Then he explained to the puzzled visitor that he had had the photograph made by a photographer who used professional models and that he kept the picture in his office for a special purpose.

"I write a lot of letters," he said, "to shareholders, customers, suppliers, and employees. I rarely know the people I write to, so when I write I look at the picture and pick out one of the people and pretend it's the person I'm writing to. It helps me get some warmth and feeling into my letter. Business letters can be awfully cold if you forget you're writing to real, live human beings."

Good story. It's probably not true, but that's not important. What *is* important is that the sentiments it expresses are admirable.

What the company president sought was a common ground on which to meet his reader. In that instance, the common ground was simple humanity, which is to say recognition of the reader as a real person.

Good public speakers almost always open their speeches with remarks calculated to establish a common ground. I recall writing a speech for the president of a large Atlanta-based company to deliver to an organization of Chicago business executives. In his opening lines my speaker made the obligatory statement about what a pleasure it was to be in Chicago. Then he paused and said, "As you know, I'm from Atlanta; and in Atlanta we call Chicago the *other* city that works."

The laughter and applause showed that my speaker had established a common ground with his audience. The common ground was, first, the humor of the remark; second, the fact that the speaker knew enough about Chicago to know that it is often called "the city that works"; and, third, the implication that he had the same pride in his city that Chicagoans had in theirs. He continued to build on his opening by mentioning some things that Atlanta and Chicago have in common.

Some people would call this building rapport with an audience. I call it finding a common ground: different words, same sentiment.

I often write speeches for executives. In my interview with the person for whom I'm writing, I always try to learn what he or she has in common with the people who will compose the audience. I dislike writing a "stock" speech — a speech that might be delivered by one of several people or to more than one audience – because I do not believe that I can find a common ground unless I know something about both the speaker and the audience.

Presidents usually begin their speeches with "My fellow Americans" or something similar. What they are saying is, in effect, *Even though I am President, I'm meeting you on a common ground — the pride we share in being Americans.*

When you write, the first step in establishing a common meeting ground with your reader is to use language that both you and the reader are comfortable with. This means resisting the use of professional jargon to communicate with people who are not members of your profession. This goes beyond the question of whether the reader will know the meanings of words. If I read an article written by an attorney for other attorneys, I might know most of the words — including the Latin phrases that attorneys like to use — but I would not necessarily feel comfortable reading the material. That's because the writer was not meeting me on any common ground. I would know that the article was not written for me.

Nothing is wrong with an attorney's writing that way to other attorneys, but if the attorney wrote that way to a client, the communication probably would not achieve what was intended.

Following is a one-sentence paragraph from a letter an accounting firm sent to partners (non-accountants) in a real estate venture. Except for the name of the partnership, the passage is real and is printed verbatim.

In our opinion, subject to the effects on the financial statements of such adjustments, if any, as might have been required had the outcome of the uncertainty about the recoverability and classification of recorded asset amounts and the amounts and classification of liabilities referred to in the preceding paragraph been known, the financial assets referred to in the first paragraph present fairly the assets, liabilities and partners' deficiencies of Green Belt Partners, Ltd. as of December 31, 1987, and its revenues for the year then ended, on the basis of Note 1, which basis has been applied in a manner consistent with that of the preceding year.

Remember, now, that this letter went to the accounting firm's clients, not to other accountants. Do you think the writer made an effort to meet his readers on common ground? The meaning of the words is not in question. I know the meaning of every word in the paragraph, but I had great difficulty in deciphering it. I'm not certain, but I think it means:

> We believe that the statements referred to in the first paragraph of this letter reflect accurately the financial condition of Green Belt Partners, Ltd. as of December 31, 1987. However, the status of certain recorded assets of the partnership is uncertain, and our opinion is subject to change if any adjustments in the financial statements should be necessary.

Some accountants, lawyers, engineers, and physicians will tell you that they must write the way the accounting firm wrote, in order to be precise. Don't believe it. People write like that to *avoid* the common ground that is so important to effective communications. They don't *want* laymen to understand their special language and thus enter their special world. "Bafflegab" is too often the language of the professions for the same reason that French was once the favored language of the English court: to set the nobility apart from the masses.

It is possible to write with precision and still write clearly and concisely. Many lawyers, accountants, and other professionals do — without worrying about letting laymen in on their secrets. *How Plain English Works for Business*, a book published by the United States Department of Commerce, gives twelve case studies of how corporations have adopted everyday English for use in promissory notes, consumer-information guides, insurance policies, and other materials. Before-and-after comparisons are remarkable.

I reject the notion that writing on technical subjects must be incomprehensible to nontechnical readers. Consider the following excerpt from an article in *Engineering News-Record*, a generally well-written magazine:

> The wind tunnel analysis developed by Rowen Williams Davies Irvin Inc., Guelph, Ontario, involved 36 different wind directions. It showed that the maximum east-west base overturning moments are caused by wind blowing along north-south alignment.

The core shear walls in the tower's lower floors handle much of the lateral loading with shear-frame interaction. There are four main shear walls — two I shapes and two C shapes — on a typical floor. These interact with the perimeter columns and perimeter spandrel beams through girders that span from the core to the perimeter.

I don't pretend to understand that passage either, but the writing is not purposely obscure. It was intended for people who know terms like *spandrel beams, core shear walls,* and *shear-frame interaction.* Its sentences are direct, relatively short, and properly constructed. It is easy to read, and it holds my attention even though I don't know all the terms.

The contrast between the passage from *Engineering News-Record* and the paragraph from the accountants' report to the partners of Green Belt is striking. In the latter I knew all the words but understood nothing; in the former I knew only half the words but understood generally what the passage meant.

Sigmund Freud, the father of psychoanalysis, was known for his ability to write clear, understandable German. I wonder how many modern psychologists can write clearly about their profession — in German *or* English.

ADULT TO ADULT

I recall reading a memorandum, written by an executive of a large company, on the subject of telephone courtesy. Now, telephone courtesy is a subject worthy of a top executive's attention because it can affect the company's image. But this memo sounded as if it came from a father admonishing his kids to be good little boys and girls. Recently I received a letter from a company that seemed out to persuade me to use its lawn-care service because its owners "deserved" a share of my business and because "the big boys" made it tough for "the little fellow" to make a living. Neither the executive's telephone-courtesy memo nor the lawn-care company's sales pitch gave the impression of being an adult-to-adult communication. Therein lies a point worth exploring.

In the 1950s a psychiatrist named Eric Berne developed a concept that became known as transactional analysis (TA) — a method of explaining and treating behavioral problems. Dr. Berne wrote a popular book on the subject entitled *Games People*

Play. A decade or so later, a protegé of Dr. Berne's, Dr. Thomas A. Harris, brought out another, more readable, book on the subject — *I'm OK — You're OK.*

The theory of transactional analysis is that the human personality is composed of three discrete elements called the *child,* the *parent,* and the *adult.* At any given time, one of these elements might be dominant. Any *transaction,* which is to say any contact between two people, is affected by the dominant element. A written contact can be a transaction just as a face-to-face contact can. The dominant element might be revealed in the tone of a memo or letter.

To understand the three personality elements — or behavioral states, as they are called — consider the following three statements:

> If the people in the office weren't so noisy, I could get my work done without having to stay late every night.
>
> If you would just plan a little better, you could get your work done on time.
>
> I suggest you close your office door when there's a distraction so that you won't be disturbed.

No doubt you already discerned that the *child* was the dominant personality of the speaker in the first sentence. In the second, the *parent* was dominant, and in the third it was the *adult.*

The tone of the first is whiny. The speaker is blaming others for his failure to complete his work on time. He plays for sympathy by mentioning he has to work late. All very childish.

The tone of the second — the *parent* statement — is clearly the I-told-you-so-why-don't-you-do-it-right tone that a parent might use with an errant child.

The third statement sounds very adult. It offers a reasonable solution to the problem.

No one likes to hear another person whine, make excuses, or blame others for his own foibles. No one likes to be scolded, lectured to, or treated as if he were six years old. Most people respond to reasonable, straightforward communications. When they are addressed as adults by adults, they react as adults should react. Keeping the principles of transactional analysis in mind as you write will help ensure that your writing has an adult-to-adult tone.

BY THE NUMBERS

Attempts have been made over the years to measure readability. One of the best-known of these attempts — possibly it was the first — was invented by the late Robert Gunning, a writing consultant. It had, if nothing else, the benefit of a clever name — the Fog Index. According to Mr. Gunning, the Fog Index was based on research from the 1920s. He introduced the Index to the world in *The Technique of Clear Writing.*

The premise of the Fog Index is that readability depends on two factors — sentence length and word length. Although this premise is a bit simplistic, there's no doubt that short words and sentences do make writing easier to read. Bernstein's concept of one idea to a sentence seems to confirm the logic of Gunning's thesis, at least to the extent that one-idea sentences are shorter sentences.

Here, from one of Mr. Gunning's later books, are instructions for applying the Fog Index to a sample of writing:

1. Find the average number of words per sentence. Use a sample of at least 100 words. Divide the total number of words by the number of sentences. This gives you average sentence length.

2. Count the number of words of three syllables or more per 100 words. Don't count: (a) words that are capitalized; (b) combinations of short, easy words — like "bookkeeper"; (c) verbs that are made three syllables by adding "ed" or "es" — like "created" or "trespasses."

3. Add the two figures above and multiply by 0.4. This will give you the Fog Index. It corresponds roughly with the number of years of schooling a person would require to read a passage with ease and understanding. [From *More Effective Writing in Business and Industry.*]

In the late 1950s, Rudolph Flesch, a teacher, an attorney, and the author of several books on writing, introduced another system for measuring readability. Dr. Flesch's system is a little more difficult to apply than Gunning's. It measures readability, not in concrete terms such as the number of years of education required to read a given passage, but on a scale of descriptive criteria from "formal" to "very popular."

From Flesch's book *A New Way to Better English*, here are instructions for applying his readability yardstick:

To test your writing . . . count off exactly 100 words as a sample.

You'll run into a few questions as to what is a word. As a rule of thumb, count everything as a word that has white space on either side. Therefore, count the article "a" as a word, and the letter "a" in enumerations, and all numbers, abbreviations, etc. (Examples: "1958," "G.O.P.," "½," "Ph.D.," "e.g.") If an abbreviation point falls in the middle of a word, count it as one word, not two. Also count as one word contractions and hyphenated words, for instance, "don't," "I've," "half-baked," "pseudo-science." . . . Now you are ready for the test count. Start again at the beginning and count one point for each of the following items:

1. Any word with a capital letter in it.

2. Any word that is underlined or italicized.

3. All numbers (unless spelled out).

4. All punctuation marks except commas, hyphens, and abbreviation points. (Periods, colons, semicolons, question marks, exclamation points, quotation marks, parentheses, brackets, apostrophes, etc.)

5. All other symbols, such as #, $, ¢, %, &.

6. One extra point for the beginning and ending of a paragraph.

If you have taken a 100-word sample, the sum total of your points is your score. If you have taken several 100-word samples, add up the points in all the samples and divide by the number of samples. The result is your average score for the whole piece of writing. . . .

Your score is likely to be somewhere between 10 and 50. Here is what it means:

Up to 20	Formal
21 to 25	Informal
26 to 30	Fairly Popular
31 to 35	Popular
Over 35	Very Popular

Formal writing, according to Flesch, is found in academic and scientific journals, *informal* in "quality" magazines such as

Harper's, fairly popular in mass-circulation fiction and nonfiction magazines, and *very popular* in mass-circulation fiction magazines.

Let's apply the Gunning and Flesch formulas to some writing samples, which I selected at random from books in my library. The first is from *Economics Explained,* by Robert Heilbroner and Lester Thurow:

> Taken together, the shift to services, the fall in mining output, and the sag in construction account for one third of our total drop in productivity over the past few decades. Thus there are obviously other industries and other reasons behind the productivity problem. Here we are going to zero in on one and only one of these additional explanations. It is the failure of American industry to invest in enough modern capital equipment to stay abreast of its Western partners. Capital equipment alone is certainly not the secret of productivity, but it is a very important part of the problem, as we shall see.
>
> This brings us back, initially, to cars and steel. Why did these industries fare so badly, vis-à-vis their international competitors? One reason is simply a failure of American management to make correct decisions. The steel industry decided not to go into oxygenation and continuous casting, and the auto industry decided not to abandon the big car. Both decisions were terribly wrong, particularly because our international competition decided otherwise.
>
> The result is that in 1980, for the first time, Japan actually produced more cars than did the United States (5.5 million against 4.5 million), and Toyota and Nissan have replaced Ford as GM's first-ranking competitors. Meanwhile, the following chart shows that the United States has trailed the entire world in converting its steel plants into continuous casting, while foreign companies ploughed their earnings back into steel.

Following Flesch's instructions, I count 259 words in that passage, which is 2.59 "samples." Under Flesch's system it scores 37 points, or 14.3 points per sample. That puts it in the "formal" category (academic and scientific journals).

The passage contains 13 sentences; average length, 19.9 words. It has 16.2 three-syllable words per 100. Applying the Fog Index formula, we get 14.4. This, according to Gunning, means that a person would have to have 14.4 years of education to read and understand the passage. That's about midway to a bachelor's degree.

My guess is that Flesch's "formal" designation is the equivalent of 14 or 15 on the Fog Index. If that's so, then the two systems rate the Heilbroner-Thurow passage about the same in terms of readability.

Let's test another piece of writing, this one from Beryl Markham's beautifully written book about Africa, *West With the Night*:

> No matter how elaborate the safari on which Makula is engaged as a tracker, he goes about naked from the waist up, carrying a quiver full of poisoned arrows. He has seen the work of the best rifles white men have yet produced, but when Makula's nostrils distend after either a good shot or a bad shot, it is not the smell of gunpowder that distends them; it is a kind of restrained contempt for that noisy and unwieldy piece of machinery with its devilish tendency to knock the untutored huntsman flat on his buttocks every time he pulls the trigger.
>
> Safaris come and safaris go, but Makula goes on forever. I suspect at times that he is one of wisest men I have ever known — so wise that, realizing the scarcity of wisdom, he has never cast a scrap of it away, though I still remember a remark he made to an overzealous newcomer to his profession: "White men pay for danger — we poor ones cannot afford it. Find your elephant, then vanish, so that you may live to find another."
>
> Makula always vanished. He went ahead in the bush with the silence of a shade, missing nothing, and the moment he had brought hunters in sight of the elephant, he disappeared with the silence of a shade, missing everything.

That is a fine piece of writing, especially the last paragraph. It has 228 words, scores 11.4, or *formal*, by the Flesch method. On the Fog Index, it scores 15.4, which means a first-quarter senior in college could read and understand it. Again, Flesch and Gunning are remarkably close to consensus. With both systems, the Markham piece shows up as slightly more difficult than the piece on economics. The Markham piece has longer sentences, but the economics piece has more three-syllable words.

Are these readability measurement systems reliable as means of targeting your writing? They certainly cannot be called scientific even though they probably are research-based. Many factors other than the ones the two systems make most use of can affect readability. Even so, their essential message cannot be denied: Shorter words, shorter sentences, shorter paragraphs, and better punctuation do make writing more reader-friendly. None of these factors, however, invariably results in "good" writing.

Both Gunning and Flesch offer some advice that is worth heeding. Here is Gunning's:

> Writing is too closely linked with life to be encased in a system. No one can say for sure what writing will succeed. You can't make rules about writing because rules are a substitute for thought — and you can't write without thinking. Therefore, don't try to write by formula alone. . . . The way to write clearly is to apply principles, not rules, of clear statement.

And this is Flesch's:

> [T]here is one more rule — a rule that's probably more important than all the others: *Don't take any of these rules too seriously.* Don't try to write mechanically to fill a set quota of capitals, periods, or quotation marks. . . . Don't strain every nerve to be relaxed and informal.

Before you start to write, think about your readers — who they are, what you want them to do or not to do or believe or feel as a result of what you write. Ask yourself how much or how little your readers know about the subject. Decide on the appropriate tone for your writing.

After you have written, read what you have written and try to see it from your reader's point of view. Have you met your reader on common ground? Have you used the right amount of informality? Is your writing an adult-to-adult communication?

Then, it can't hurt — and it might help — to test your writing by either Gunning or Flesch.

6.
Overcoming Writer's Block

*Writing is easy. All you have to do is
stare at a blank sheet of paper until
drops of blood form on your forehead.*
— Gene Fowler (1890-1960)

Today a writer is more likely to stare at a blank computer screen
than a blank sheet of paper, but the drops of blood that form on
the writer's forehead are not high-tech blood. They're the same
kind that formed on Fowler's forehead when he sat down at his
typewriter.

Fowler's droll reference to blood was in fact an admission that
he was susceptible to an affliction everyone — from the most
seasoned pro to the rankest amateur — suffers from now and
then: writer's block.

What is writer's block? What is it about writing that turns the
mind to mush? That makes irresistible any slight temptation to
put off starting to write? That makes writers wish they had taken
up plumbing or accounting or crop dusting or brain surgery?

You may be surprised to know that writer's block is an organizational problem. Think about it. I doubt that you often sit down
to write without having a good idea of what you want to say. If
you can't seem to get started, it's probably because you can't
decide what to say first.

Overcoming writer's block is partly a matter of training. Newspaper reporters, for example, are trained to write fast. They
couldn't meet their deadlines if they had to agonize over how to

start every story. Their training includes techniques for organizing a news story. Good reporters usually don't have to think much about what comes first. If they know the subject, they know what is most important, and that is what they select as the "lead." Pick up a newspaper and read the lead paragraphs of several stories — news stories, not features, editorials, or opinion columns. You'll see that they follow a pattern.

This chapter on overcoming writer's block is mostly a discussion of organizational techniques. The better you are at organizing material, the less blood will form on your forehead when you sit down to write.

START WITH AN OUTLINE

Before you begin to write anything other than a routine letter or memo, make an outline. Even short items are easier to write after you have taken a few minutes to think about and jot down the points you want to make. Making an outline forces you to think through a writing problem. Once the outline is complete, it gives you confidence.

An outline need not be — *should* not be — too detailed or too elaborate. Nor should it be chiseled in stone. If you become too engrossed in making an outline, you could fall victim to "outline block," which means you might become so concerned with the form of your outline that the outline itself becomes the problem rather than the solution.

I disagree with teachers who require students to "turn in" their outlines. An outline is valuable only to its originator. If the writing in the final piece is good, the quality and form of the outline are irrelevant. If the writing is bad, however, the teacher might suspect that the student has not learned the importance of outlining and might be justified in asking to see outlines in future assignments.

SIMPLE FORMAT FOR OUTLINING

A formal outline of the type usually associated with academic papers probably would take so much time to prepare that it would defeat its purpose if you tried to use it for most business writing. I suggest developing a simple format that suits your writing style and the kinds of things you write. Here is a format that I sometimes use. It might work for you:

WHY AM I WRITING?

WHO ARE MY READERS?

WHAT DO I WANT TO HAPPEN?

WHAT IS THE MAIN IDEA I WANT TO GET ACROSS?

WHAT ARE THE MAJOR SUPPORTING FACTS?

WHAT ARE THE MINOR SUPPORTING FACTS?

That, strictly speaking, is not even an outline format. But for me it serves the same purpose: It gets me started. It forces me to answer the questions that must be answered before I can write. If it suits you, fine; if not, roll your own.

THE FIVE W'S

Another good technique for getting started is to apply the Five W's, a formula said to have originated in a journalism textbook published late in the 19th century. The author of that textbook suggested the Five W's — who, what, when, where, and why — as a guide to remind young reporters of the information that should be in the opening paragraph of a news story.

Some instructors insist on throwing in how, making it Five W's and an H; but that offends my sense of order, so I stick with the original version.

Generations of journalists — cubs and veterans alike — have used the Five W's not only as a reminder but also as a "starter." You can use them when you write letters, memos, reports, and other business communications. Ask yourself:

WHO will read this communication?
WHO will be affected by the information?

WHAT is the purpose of this communication?
WHAT do I want to tell my readers?
WHAT do I want them to do?

WHEN do I want my readers to react to the communication?
WHEN did or will the activity take place?

WHERE did or will the event take place?

WHERE can the reader obtain more information?

WHY do I believe the readers will be or should be interested in the information?

Write down the answers to these and other relevant questions and you'll have most if not all the information you need to complete the task.

The Five W's are also a device for testing your writing to determine whether it is complete.

THINK FIRST DRAFT

Once you have your outline and you're ready to start, think *first draft*. What you write first does not have to be the final version. You don't have to get it right the first time. If you adopt this attitude, you won't be as susceptible to writer's block. So what if everything's not perfect? You'll have another crack at it. You might find it helpful to carry this concept a step further and think of the first draft as little more than an outline. This, of course, will depend on your own work habits, the nature of the writing assignment, and how much time you have to work on it.

Start anywhere. Get it down in chronological order if that's the way it wants to come out. Or start at what might seem to be the end and work backward to the beginning. Momentum is the most important thing about first-draft writing. Whatever it takes to keep the work moving, do it. If you lack a fact or a figure you need, leave a blank and fill it in later. If you don't know how to spell a word or if you're not sure you have the exact word you need, don't stop to look it up. You can do that on the second draft.

If you're working on something you can't complete in one sitting — for example, a speech, a magazine article, or a long report — here's a way to "jump-start" your writing engine when you return after a hiatus: Go back several paragraphs or even several pages and start by copying what you have written. You'll find that by the time you reach the point where you stopped, you're off and running again. I've used this technique many times. It works. I sometimes stop writing in the middle of a sentence, knowing that trying to recall what I had planned to say in that sentence will help me get restarted.

THE INVERTED PYRAMID

Another journalistic technique is an organizational pattern called "the inverted pyramid." This is a method of organizing a news story so that (1) the most important fact is at the beginning and (2) each subsequent fact is less important than the one immediately preceding. By the time you get near the end of a story written in the inverted pyramid style, you're into "throw-away" lines. This has been likened to starting a joke with the punch line or a whodunit with who did it.

Nevertheless, the inverted pyramid makes reading a newspaper article more efficient. The reader can concentrate on the first few paragraphs and skim over the remainder without missing much. The pattern, however, probably was not developed with the reader in mind. Most likely it evolved as the solution to a mechanical problem. When newspapers were printed from metal type, everything had to fit perfectly in order for the "form" to "lock up." If a story was a little too long to fit the "hole" allotted to it, someone would have to decide how to shorten it. If the story was organized in an inverted pyramid, the printer usually could cut it from the bottom without having to consult the editor or the reporter who wrote the story. Cutting material from anywhere else in a story would mean the copy would have to go back to the linotype machine for expensive and time-consuming typesetting.

Whatever its origin, the inverted pyramid survives in modern journalism, and it can be used to the advantage of both the writer and the reader in certain types of business communications. Like busy newspaper-readers, busy memo-readers appreciate getting essential facts early so they can decide whether to stop reading, to continue reading for more details, or perhaps to skim the remainder.

In practice, you'll probably prefer to modify the inverted pyramid style for your own short, routine memos.

SECOND DRAFT: TIME TO GET SERIOUS

As I mentioned at the beginning of this discussion, you'll find it easier to get started if you keep in mind that you're not writing the final draft. But, let's face it, you will write the final draft eventually. Once you've completed the first draft — after you've got it all out of your head and on paper — it's time to get serious. Let's say you've read what you've written and you're satisfied that all the information is there. The next thing you must do is put it all in the right order. You might be unsure how to go about organizing it, especially if it's a long piece.

When this happens to me I often use a technique I call the "grad-school method." It's akin to a technique commonly used by students preparing to write research papers. The student puts each item of information on a separate index card. This enables the student to move cards around to arrive at a logical order. The result is a sort of "skeleton" of the article. Then all that remains is to put some meat on the bones.

To use the grad-school method with your own second drafts, take a pair of scissors and cut your copy into strips of one paragraph each. Lay the strips on a table and move paragraphs around to see how they work in different locations. When you're satisfied with the order, write the necessary connectives. If you write on a word processor you can move paragraphs around easily. However, I still prefer a hard copy of my writing when I use the grad-school method to reorganize.

Remember, even the best writers rarely get by with only one draft. Most professionals write at least two — often three or more — before they're satisfied. Someone has said that there is no good writing, only good *rewriting*. Believe it.

I find it helpful to put writing aside for awhile before revising. I believe in the power of the unconscious mind to solve problems the conscious mind is incapable of solving. In my experience, writing problems often have seemed to solve themselves overnight — literally. This has happened too often to be coincidental.

LIST IT

When you have to write a piece that discusses several items, consider presenting the material in list form rather than in narrative. For example, if you're reporting on a meeting in which several things were discussed, you might want to handle it something like this:

At the board meeting, directors discussed the following:
— Proposed acquisition of Acme Manufacturing Co.;
— Appointment of new auditing firm;
— Election of Robert Jones as executive vice president;
— Closing of the company's Mississippi plant; and
— The purchase of a new mainframe computer for the home office.

Each item in the list could then be discussed individually with several sentences or even paragraphs devoted to it. This is a much more efficient way to present the information than to write it in narrative form. The reader can glance at the list, take in the essential points, and decide whether he wants the details. It is reader-friendly. A memo presenting information of this type using only narrative could be awkward, especially if the writer felt compelled to introduce each new item with a phrase like *Another important item discussed.*

In listing information, resist the temptation to toss in an item that is not of the same grammatical form as the others. For example, in the above memo you should not write something like **Board Chairman Smith proposed the election of Robert Jones as executive vice president** instead of **Election of Robert Jones as executive vice president,** because it is "out of sync" with the others. It does not go with ... **directors discussed the following.**

TELL, SELL, AND SOFTEN

Many business communications fall into one of three categories: communications that provide information; communications designed to sell, convince, or persuade; and communications that convey bad news such as a refusal, a criticism, or a price increase. I call these communications that tell, sell, or soften. Knowing the essential ingredients of each can make writing them easier.

Communications That Tell. These are routine letters, memos, and bulletins designed simply to inform. Here are some ways to make them more effective:

1. Keep them short and direct.

2. Put the most important point in the first sentence.

3. Organize the remainder of the message in the inverted pyramid style.

4. Use the Five W's as a reminder to include all the necessary information.

5. Be certain the tone of the memo is appropriate to the intended audience.

Communications That Sell. These are a real challenge even for the best writers. Some of the most effective writing is found in sales letters. A good sales letter grabs the reader's attention from the beginning, holds it as long as necessary to make all the pertinent points, and leads the reader to the desired decision. To induce a person to write a check and send off an order for a product he has not seen — all on the basis of an unsolicited letter — must be quite an accomplishment. Yet it happens every day.

You may never have to write a sales letter, but if you do, here are some suggestions for making it more effective:

1. Open with a device to get the reader's attention. One or more of the following might be appropriate:
   (a) Offer a benefit or an inducement.
   (b) Involve the reader in some way.
   (c) Include some type of gimmick or an item such as a coin, a stamp, or a pencil.
   (d) Make a startling statement or give a surprising statistic.
   (e) Ask a rhetorical question.

2. Use the body of the letter to:
   (a) Show *how* the product or proposal you are selling will benefit the reader.
   (b) Explain exactly what you have in mind.
   (c) Emphasize the main features of the product or proposal.

3. Near the end of the letter:
   (a) Ask the reader for a specific action (e.g., send in the order, telephone, etc.).
   (b) Remind the reader of the benefit.
   (c) Create a sense of urgency.

4. Throughout the letter:
   (a) Write with the reader's point of view in mind.
   (b) Make each word, each sentence, each paragraph lead to

the next. If you lose the reader early in the letter, you'll have little chance of getting him back.

(c) Make your writing positive and energetic.

(d) Apply the principles of good writing as described by the Five C's.

The next time you receive a sales letter, note how many of these suggestions it follows. Even if you never have occasion to write a letter to sell a product, you'll probably write many letters to persuade someone to do something — make a charitable contribution, support a political candidate, grant an interview. Most such communications should include some of the elements of a good sales letter.

Communications That Soften. Few people take pleasure in conveying bad news. When we must convey bad news we do so as gently as we can. In business communications bad news must be conveyed in such a way as to leave the recipient with a good impression of you and your company. This is kindness, not hypocrisy. It is also good business.

Here are some suggestions to help you to write a gracious letter of refusal or unwelcome news:

1. Open your letter by pointing out some area of agreement or by giving the reader a *sincere* compliment. This almost certainly will signal the reader that the bad news is coming, but it will assure him that you take no pleasure in it.

2. Give facts and rationale to support or explain your position.

3. State the bad news in positive terms if you can. Rather than **Your shipment will have to be delayed until June 1,** you might write **We will ship your order no later than June 1.** Statements like this should be realistic. Promising or implying something that's not likely to occur is the worst thing you can do.

4. Use an adult-to-adult tone. Don't be reluctant to apologize if you or your company has erred; but don't be too contrite over an honest mistake. Explain the reasons for the mistake and tell how you will correct it. Don't be defensive.

5. Be aware that what you say in a letter could cause legal problems for your company. This is especially important in matters involving job applicants.

EXERCISE 11: BREAKING BAD NEWS

For this exercise, pretend that you recently have been put in charge of community relations for a company that has plants in several small cities. Each year for the past five years, one of the plants has allowed a community service organization to use a vacant warehouse to hold a fund-raising event. The organization uses the money it raises to support a local orphanage. You have just received a letter from Mrs. Arnold, president of the group, announcing the date of the next fund-raiser. Obviously, she assumes there is no question that your company will allow the group to use the facility. However, the company's legal counsel and its safety director have decreed otherwise: They have informed you that they cannot permit the practice to continue.

The event has become popular in the community, and each year attendance has increased. For two years, the safety director has expressed concern about fire safety with so many people in the warehouse, but he has been reluctant to prohibit its use, because of the importance of maintaining good relations with the community. This year, the legal counsel has done so on the ground that the company is leaving itself vulnerable to a lawsuit.

The buck has passed to you. You have no choice but to inform Mrs. Arnold of the company's decision. Your schedule precludes delivery of the bad news in person, so you decide to write a letter.

Which of the following would you choose as the opening of the letter?

Dear Mrs. Arnold:

Our company has supported your organization for the past several years by allowing you to use our warehouse for your fundraiser. I am sure you will agree that we have gone "above and beyond" the call of duty in exercising our responsibility to the community.

Dear Mrs. Arnold:

I am sorry to be the one to inform you that your organization has been denied the privilege to use our warehouse for this year's fund-raiser. I want you to know that this is not my decision. It is something decided by the "powers that be," namely our legal counsel and our safety director.

Dear Mrs. Arnold:

I recently became manager of community relations for our company, and my predecessor told me about the fine work your organization is doing to support the orphanage. Our company is proud of the small part we have been able to play in that work. For this reason, I'm especially sorry to tell you that we cannot permit the annual fund-raiser to be held in our facility this year.

Choose one of the three openers and complete the letter according to the suggestions for writing communications to convey bad news. If none of the three suits you, write your own.

7.
Some Do's, Don'ts, and Why Nots

Be not the first by whom the new are tried,
Nor yet the last to lay the old aside.
— Alexander Pope

One reason linguists study Latin — other than the fact of its enormous influence on other languages — is that it is a "dead" language and therefore never changes. English, on the other hand, changes constantly. Spoken English changes faster than written English, but changes in the spoken language, if they are used persistently, find their way eventually into writing.

A black friend of mine who shares with me a fascination for language once told me that he is amused by whites, and some blacks, who affect so-called black English. Outsiders can't speak black English, he said, because it changes so fast that by the time an outsider thinks he knows what a word means, it might mean something else. Thus, the outsider is always a step or two behind. It seems to me that the same could be said of other types of "street talk," neighborhood slang, and the speech with which teenagers confound their parents and their teachers.

If this is true, then the reason these speech patterns *can* change as fast as they do is that they are not written; therefore, they are free of the constraints that writing imposes on language. Stated another way, writing prevents language from changing too fast and thus becoming less effective as a medium of communication.

Writers, particularly professional writers, are in a sense custodians of language. Just as a sensible person does not buy a new wardrobe with every fashion fad, a sensible writer does not eagerly accept every word fad, every neologism, and every departure from conventional grammar. In both fashion and writing, a prudent person will heed the advice of Alexander Pope.

If language changed too fast, it would recreate the Tower of Babel; too slowly, it would stultify; and it would not be flexible enough to accommodate new technologies and new mores. Consider, for example, the problems of using Latin to write about computers or nuclear energy. This, incidentally, is a real problem for the Vatican: The Catholic Church's encyclicals, written in Latin, apply ancient and eternal wisdom to modern problems.

Rules, or what is called *prescriptive grammar*, help to regulate the pace of change, and that is why the rules of grammar and the accepted norms of usage should not be ignored without good reason. In this chapter I give my opinion on some perplexing questions of usage and my reasons for those opinions. Experts on usage differ on many of the questions discussed. In each instance I consulted two or more authorities to find support for my opinions. Consulting experts on grammar and usage is habitual with me. It should be habitual with anyone who writes.

LAUGH AND BE GAY

The processes that cause language to change are natural, not forced. Attempts to force new words into the language or to assign new meanings to old words are rarely successful. Changes usually become permanent when they fill a need. Often they add richness and diversity.

The word *gay*, meaning *homosexual*, is an example. Its use has become widespread as a result of society's changed attitude toward homosexuality. "Gay rights" advocates have pushed for acceptance of *gay* in that sense, but it's doubtful their efforts would have succeeded had there been no legitimate need for another way to say *homosexual*. In these times of informality in speech and writing, *homosexual* seems too clinical for most people to use comfortably, but gutter characterizations such as *queer* and *pansy* are distasteful to sensitive people. *Gay*, therefore, enables ordinary people to discuss homosexuality in ordinary conversation. It takes homosexuality out of the linguistic closet.

Gay is a euphemism, which is by definition a "pleasant" word or phrase used in place of a harsher one. *Pass away* for *die* is an example. Some writers object to *gay* for the reason that they object to other euphemisms: A euphemism tends to convey incorrect information about whatever it describes. Those who object to *gay* on that ground believe that it obscures the true nature of homosexuality and thereby inhibits clear communication. Be that as it may, the word is with us, probably forever; and generations of English speakers yet unborn may never know it was ever in question.

I think it regrettable that the traditional meaning of *gay* seems destined to become archaic. After all, who could sing "My Old Kentucky Home" without choking on "It's summer, the old folks are gay."

To the question of whether *gay* should be used in writing, the answer must be "Why not?" If it makes you uncomfortable, use homosexual, but be aware that the new meaning is here to stay. Accept it.

THE HE'S AND SHE'S

Traditional English requires a masculine pronoun or pronominal adjective (*he, him,* or *his*) with a singular antecedent when the gender of the antecedent is unspecified. **A doctor must respect HIS patients if HE wants them to respect HIM** is correct even though a doctor can be either a woman or a man. Those who defend traditional usage say that *his, he,* and *him* are not gender-specific when used in that way. Those who believe it is time to scrap traditional usage say that it perpetuates the myth of male superiority. They also say, not without justification, that using the masculine pronouns implies that some professions are exclusively for men, others for women.

Consider what happens when you substitute *nurse* for *doctor* in the example above: **A nurse must respect HIS patients if HE wants them to respect HIM.** Doesn't sound right, does it? That's because the vast majority of nurses are women. But there are many male nurses, and there are many female doctors. Until recently, most writers would have thought nothing amiss about the sentence with *doctor,* but they invariably would have written **A nurse must respect HER patients ...** instead of **A nurse must respect HIS patients ...**

All this illustrates one of the most perplexing problems facing writers today: sexism, real or imaginary. No writer should be insensitive to sexist language, but few are willing to use the clumsy and often dissonant alternatives that have been suggested.

In many instances, a sentence can be recast to eliminate the problem. When that option is available, it's probably the best. Thus, **A DOCTOR must respect HIS patients** becomes **DOCTORS must respect THEIR patients.** Presto! Problem gone. But if a writer has to recast all his sentences in that way, he gives up a certain amount of flexibility. Many writers feel it restricts their ability to achieve style and grace and variety in their writing.

What's a writer to do? How can you eliminate sexism from your writing without sacrificing flexibility of style? I don't know whether anyone has a good answer to that question. I have some thoughts to share with you.

He or she isn't bad if it's not overused. I use *he or she* early in a piece of writing to establish the fact that I'm referring to either sex. Afterward, I use it now and then when it seems natural. Most often, I use the traditional masculine pronoun for gender-less constructions. This is the practice I have adopted for this book. Overuse of *he or she* can result in such monstrosities as **He or she must decide for himself or herself what is best; otherwise he or she can never be his or her own person.**

The "slash" solution is the worst of a collection of bad ideas. This is the use of *he/she, him/herself,* and the like. To the sensitive ear, it has about the same effect as scratching on a blackboard.

And then there's the "equal time" solution. I read a business book in which the author took pains to alternate *he* and *she* lest anyone get the idea that he (the author, who is a man) did not believe women could be managers. Reading the book, I felt as if I were watching a tennis match. I was so conscious of the writing that I lost interest in the subject. I wondered whether the he-and-she references would come out even or, if not, which gender would get the extra point. Then it occurred to me that a writer who was really interested in equality would count the number of personal pronouns in the book and use *he* and *she* with a frequency equal to the percentage that each gender is to the population.

The singular pronoun *everyone* or *everybody* is often paired with the plural *their* or *they*, as in **EVERYONE must make up THEIR own mind.** This usage is common in speech, even in the speech of educated people such as television news anchors. It is *not*, however, standard English. In my opinion, it will be — and not too long hence — an accepted idiom in all but the most pedantic writing. I say this for two reasons: First, it *sounds* natural; it scarcely raises an eyebrow, let alone a hackle. Second, it is *logical;* we tend to think of *everybody* or *everyone* as a collective that means, not one person, but all people.

Should you use constructions like **Everyone must make up their own mind?** No. Remember Pope's advice. Wait until such usage begins to show up in *The New York Times.*

An excellent discussion of how to avoid sexist pronouns appears in Appendix B, courtesy of consultant Vee Nelson.

MORE SEX(ISM) EDUCATION

Unfortunately, expressions such as *girl photographer, female doctor,* and *lady executive* are not uncommon. Such expressions are unacceptable today. If the gender of the photographer, the doctor, or the executive is relevant, find a better way to express it.

An article in *The Atlanta Constitution* (February 22, 1988) about Jimmy Swaggart, the television evangelist who got caught with his morals down, contained a blatantly sexist sentence:

> During the emotional 90-minute church service, Swaggart apologized to his wife, Frances, who, wearing a pink dress, sat behind the altar.

If the occasion had been a fashion show, the color of Mrs. Swaggart's dress would have been relevant. Had Mrs. Swaggart been on the hot seat and her husband behind the altar, would the reporter have treated his readers to such a juicy bit of information as the color of the Rev. Mr. Swaggart's suit? I think not.

Sexism is also inherent in many common words such as *postman* and *chairman.* The question is, which of the many possible substitutes for such words are acceptable. Mail *carrier* sounds natural and is a logical substitute for *postman. Chairperson* is logical but awkward. *Chair* is neither natural nor logical. It is an affectation favored by people who insist on being oh-so-modern and socially conscious.

It is easy to make light of the problem by citing a few patently ridiculous suggestions that have been made to "neuterize" the language, such as a proposal put forth — presumably in fun — to substitute *peep* for *man* in certain compound words. *Chair-peep, peepslaughter, hupeepity,* and *peephole.* Such are good for a laugh, but there's nothing funny about the problem.

In the past few years, we have begun to see a trend away from words like *chairperson* and a return to traditional words. Nevertheless, some words ending in *man* may never regain their former status in our language.

My suggestion is to use gender-neutral nouns when you can without resorting to awkward or illogical substitutes.

ABANDON HOPEFULLY

Edwin Newman reportedly has a sign in his office that says, "Abandon hopefully, ye who enter here."

Although I doubt that Mr. Newman's office could be compared with Dante's Hades, I do *not* doubt that he would like to raise hell with anyone who uses *hopefully* in his presence — unless the person uses it as an adverb. The use of *hopefully* that gives him and others apoplexy is in sentences like **Hopefully, she will apply for the position.** In that sentence, *hopefully* means *I hope that* or *it is hoped that.* As an adverb, *hopefully* should describe the manner in which something is done. **She will apply for the job hopefully** means that she will apply for a job in a hopeful manner, presumably with hat in hand and eagerness in her eyes.

I share Mr. Newman's distaste for *hopefully.* It is an overworked word that deserves a long rest — a century should be about right. Frankly, though, I think that its use as a non-adverb is defensible. It is not a lot different from *frankly* in the previous sentence. *Fortunately* (it is fortunate that), *happily* (I am happy that), *consequently* (as a consequence), and other words seem to be adverbs but function otherwise in idiomatic speech and writing.

I don't use *hopefully* except as an adverb, and I hope that you won't; but if you do, don't use it around the venerable Edwin Newman.

CALL HER MS.

As a native Southerner, I've used *Ms.* all my life. But I always spelled it m-i-z; or I would have, if I'd had an occasion to write it. In the South the word usually goes with the *last* name of a married woman. It's the way Southerners pronounce *Mrs.* Most Southerners use *Miss* with the **first name* of a married woman *or* a single woman. Thus a native speaker of Southern probably would say either *Miz Carter* or *Miss Rosalyn,* not *Miz Rosalyn.*

But this is not a treatise on how to speak Southern, so let's get on with the business at hand.

The designation *Ms.,* whether it addresses a married woman or an unmarried woman, is useful. I recall many times having to write a letter to a woman without knowing her marital status, and wondering what salutation to use. Now that we have *Ms.,* there's no problem. I rate *Ms.* a "Do."

You should be aware that not every woman likes to be addressed as Ms. My feeling is, if you know that a woman is married, and if she uses her married name, addressing her as *Mrs.* is preferable.

Many newspapers that try scrupulously to avoid sexism and always refer to women as *Ms.* never refer to men as *Mr.* That practice, it seems to me, is itself sexist. Logic suggests that if they're going to call Mr. Jones *Jones,* they ought to call Ms. Smith *Smith.* But I suppose absolute equality is a Utopian dream.

The custom of calling actresses *Miss* has persisted. Elizabeth Taylor has remained *Miss Taylor* even while being, at various times, Mrs. Hilton, Mrs. Fisher, Mrs. Burton, and Mrs. Warner.

Other forms of address give writers trouble. *Reverend* is an adjective. As a form of address it should be used the same way as *honorable.* Thus, **the Reverend Pat Robertson** or **the Reverend Mr. Robertson** is correct. **Reverend Robertson** is *not* correct, although it is commonly used, often by the Reverend Reverends themselves. *Reverend* by itself is not a correct form of address either, any more than *Honorable* by itself.

When addressing a physician or the holder of a doctoral degree, never use both the title (*Dr.* or *Doctor*) and the degree: **James D. Kiley, M.D.,** or **Dr. James D. Kiley,** but *not* **Dr. James D. Kiley, M.D.; Miles McGinty, Ed.D,** not **Dr. Miles McGinty, Ed.D.**

I'm sure you have wondered about the proper salutation to use on a business letter when you have only the company name, not the name of a person to whom to address the letter. So have I. I've had letters beginning with *Greetings* (sounds like a draft notice), *Dear Friend* (presumptuous; my *real* friends call me by name), *Dear Sir or Madam* (noncommittal), *Good Morning* (I rarely open my mail in the morning), and *Hello* (could be a wrong number). None of the above sounds natural to me, yet I don't want to be so old-fashioned as to use *Dear Sir*. I recently wrote a letter to a bank and I used *Dear Bank* as the salutation, but it was a letter of complaint, and somehow the bank didn't seem especially dear at the time.

If you have a solution to this problem, I'd like to know about it.

WINSTON TALKED GOOD

Winston Churchill was not only a great wartime leader, he was also an accomplished user of the English language in both speech and writing. His mocking reference to the "rule" against ending a sentence with a preposition is quoted almost as often as the famous "blood, toil, tears, and sweat" speech with which he inspired Britons during World War II.

The story is, Churchill was perturbed when an editor presumed to correct a Churchillian sentence that ended with a preposition. Wrote he to the editor: "This is the sort of impertinence up with which I will not put."

The admonition against ending a sentence with a preposition is a relatively recent one. It may stem from the fact that *preposition* means *place before* (pre-position). In any case, don't hesitate to end a sentence with a preposition if doing so results in a sentence that sounds natural. If anyone objects, tell him I said that a preposition is a perfectly good word to end a sentence with.

THE LATE ADAM AND EVE

To call history's earliest couple *late* is patently absurd. People who have been dead a long time, especially well-known people, should never be referred to as late. *The late George Washington, the late Abraham Lincoln,* and even *the late Franklin D. Roosevelt* are inappropriate because everyone knows that Washington, Lincoln, and Roosevelt are deceased.

Note, however, that *the late Franklin D. Roosevelt* does not sound as ridiculous as *the late George Washington.* The longer a person has been dead, the less reason to use *late.* How long is long? I don't know. Common sense may be your best — indeed, your *only* — guide.

I do know that it is redundant to write **The late Rock Hudson, who died in 1987.** Simply **Rock Hudson, who died in 1987,** is sufficient.

ARE THE NEW YORK TIMES SOLD HERE?

Some writers are troubled by collectives, nouns that are singular in form but may take either a singular or plural verb. Examples are *group, couple, family, majority,* and *total.* The list is long.

Whether to use a singular verb form or a plural verb form with a collective depends on what the writer has in mind. Which is correct, **The couple WAS married in 1987** or **The couple WERE married in 1987?** In that instance, *were* is preferred because you're thinking of two individuals who were joined in marriage. In The couple WAS attacked as THEY walked through the park, the newspaper reporter seemed to be trying to have it both ways. *Couple* cannot be plural (they) in one part of the sentence and singular (it) in another.

In **A majority of the residents are Republicans,** the fact that *Republicans* is plural seems to mandate *are.* But in **A majority of the population is Republican,** the singular *Republican* and the singular *population* indicate that the writer is referring to the population as a unit.

The total number of employees has (singular) **increased this year,** but **A total of 14 people work** (plural) **here now.** In those examples, the controlling words are *the* and *a.* When you use the collective *total* or *number,* choose the singular verb with *the,* the plural verb with *a* or *an.*

With a collective noun such as *committee,* as in **The committee is/are well qualified to select art for the new office,** choose either the singular or the plural verb form, depending on whether you're thinking of the qualifications of the individual committee members or of the qualifications of the committee as a whole. If your meaning could as easily be expressed by **Members of the committee are well qualified** . . ., it could be stated as **The committee are well qualified** . . .

The best way to determine which verb form is appropriate is to ask yourself what you want to say to the reader. In many instances, the difference won't be worth worrying about.

Some compound subjects that are technically plural may require a singular verb form because they are thought of as almost inseparable. **Bacon and eggs is** (not *are*) **my favorite breakfast; Sears, Roebuck & Company is a huge organization,** and **Fresh air and sunshine was what he needed** are examples.

A few common words taken directly from Latin have plurals that are not formed the way plurals of most English words are formed. *Phenomena* is the plural of *phenomenon,* and *criteria* is the plural of *criterion.* Using those words in any other way is unacceptable. *Data* is plural, but because its singular, *datum,* is rarely seen except in academic or scientific writing, *data* may be used with a singular verb form as a synonym for *information.* Using *data* with a plural verb form, as in **The data are not all compiled,** seems pretentious to some people even though it is still common. It seems natural to me because that's the way I learned it. *Agenda* is plural (singular: *agendum*) but is almost always used as if it were singular. *Fora* is the plural of *forum,* but the preferred plural now is forums. By the way, if you want to make an easy five bucks, bet someone he can't tell you the plural of *opus.* You'll get *opi, opuses,* and some others. The answer is *opera.*

THE DOOM OF WHOM

Descriptive grammarians — grammarians concerned, not with "right" or "wrong," but with how a language is used by most people — have been saying for years that *whom* is doomed, that it is no longer natural in spoken English and that it is passing out of the written language except when immediately preceded by a preposition, as in *to whom* or *for whom.*

But *whom* stubbornly refuses to die. People like me help to keep it alive. I use *whom* because Miss Grundy or someone like her insisted on it. Whether it serves any useful purpose in our language is debatable.

If you want to use *who* and *whom* according to conventional grammar, you have to understand the difference between the nominative (subjective) and the objective cases. A word in the nominative case is a noun or pronoun used as the subject of a verb. A noun or pronoun used as the object of a verb or of a preposition is in the objective case. For example, in **The book is on the table,** *book* is the subject of *is* and is in the nominative case. In **I saw the book on the table,** *book* is the object of *saw* and is in the objective case. The difference between *who* and *whom* is simple: *Who* is nominative, *whom* is objective. The principle applies also to *whoever* and *whomever.*

In **That is the woman who was in the store,** *who* is the subject of *was,* which means it is in the nominative case. In **That is the woman whom I saw in the store,** *whom* is the object of *saw,* which makes it the objective case. Confusion arises, particularly in speech, when the relationship between the sentence elements is not recognized. A kind of sentence that is especially troublesome is **Please hand the package to whoever/whomever answers the door.** The preposition *to* leads many speakers and writers to choose *whomever* in such sentences in the belief that the pronoun is the object of *to.* This is an understandable error, because *to whomever* sounds natural and is correct in the prepositional phrase. The correct choice in the example, however, is *whoever* because it is the subject of *answers.*

To be consistently correct, the writer must make a habit of considering carefully the relationship of the sentence elements to each other. The same can be said of other perplexing grammatical questions. That is why Miss Grundy insisted that her pupils learn to diagram sentences. No more effective way to teach sentence structure has been devised. No one adept at diagramming has a problem with *who* and *whom.*

All this industrial strength grammar notwithstanding, you can usually ignore *whom* in speech without causing too many raised eyebrows; and you probably can do so in writing as well, except in constructions where a preposition immediately precedes the pronoun. You're not likely to be criticized much for using *who* for both the nominative and the objective. You must not, however, make the mistake of using *whom* as the nominative. That makes you sound as though you want to use the correct form but don't know how. To be blunt, it makes you sound ignorant.

My advice is to learn how to use *who* and *whom* correctly. It's really not too difficult. Maybe one day the descriptive grammarians will win the battle and *whom* will just fade away. Until then, why not show this venerable pronoun some respect?

IS IT OKAY TO SOMETIMES SPLIT AN INFINITIVE?

An infinitive is a verb preceded by *to* — e.g., *to eat, to destroy, to understand.* A "split" infinitive is an infinitive in which *to* is separated from the verb by one or more words — e.g. *to hungrily eat, to willfully destroy, to thoroughly understand.*

If splitting an infinitive now and then doesn't bother you, you're in good company — John Donne, Samuel Pepys, Daniel Defoe, Robert Burns, Samuel Taylor Coleridge, George Eliot, Arthur Conan Doyle, Rudyard Kipling, Abraham Lincoln, and a host of others. If you do not split an infinitive without first trying it unsplit, you're also in good company — Richard Dowis and a host of others.

There is little support for the notion that placing one word or more between *to* and the verb in an infinitive is a grammatical error. That notion may have come from early grammarians who tried to force English to follow the same grammatical rules as Latin. In Latin and in languages derived from it, the *to* is "built in" and cannot be separated from the verb. In Spanish, for example, *hablar* means *to speak.*

Splitting the infinitive is sometimes necessary to convey the meaning you intend. For example, in **He decided to promptly return the money he found,** *promptly* clearly relates to *return.* Moving *promptly* to another location in the sentence eliminates the split infinitive but changes the meaning. **He promptly decided to return the money he found** tells the reader that the finder *decided* promptly, but it says nothing about how long the finder will keep the money before returning it. Placing *promptly* immediately before the infinitive could leave the reader uncertain whether the word applied to *decided* or *return.* Placing it immediately after the infinitive makes it clear that *promptly* relates to *return,* but the construction seems awkward. Putting *promptly* at the end of the sentence is out of the question because it then would seem to modify *found.*

It is acceptable, though not always desirable, to place any number of qualifying words between *to* and its verb in an infinitive. **The company plans to immediately, and with as little fanfare as possible, remove the product from the market** is not incorrect, but **The company plans to remove the product from the market immediately and with as little fanfare as possible** is preferred.

In a few instances, avoiding a split infinitive is almost impossible — for example, **The chairman said he expects the company's net income to more than double this year.** In that sentence, *more than* can go no other place. Interestingly, substituting *almost* for *more than* creates a less difficult problem. In **The chairman said he expects the company's net income almost to double this year,** *almost to double* makes sense, but *to almost double* is the more natural word order.

The advice here is, don't hesitate to split an infinitive when doing so will make your meaning unmistakable or prevent an awkward construction. Otherwise, resist the temptation to split infinitives. If the practice bothers some readers, why not eliminate as many splits from your writing as you can?

DESTROY THE WICKED WHICH

Not every writer makes a distinction between *that* and *which* as relative pronouns used to introduce clauses. But there is a difference, and it is worth preserving. The difference is easily explained in grammatical terms. *That* is used to introduce a defining, or restricting, clause. In **The automobile that I saw in the parking lot is a 1987 Ford,** the clause *that I saw in the parking lot* defines the car. It says something about one particular car and no other. In **The automobile, which I saw in the parking lot, is a 1987 Ford,** the clause *which I saw in the parking lot* is a nondefining, or nonrestricting, clause. It is little more than a parenthetical expression, not necessary to the sentence. It simply provides an additional fact.

Note that the nondefining clause in the example is set off by commas, indicating natural pauses. Many grammarians, including Edward D. Johnson, whose handbook of grammar I recommend, say that the commas, not *which,* make the clause nondefining. Mr. Johnson would maintain that **The automobile *which* I saw in the parking lot** means the same as **The automobile *that* I saw in the parking lot.** Nevertheless, I will stick with the practice of using *that* to introduce defining clauses and *which* to introduce nondefining clauses. And, in my mind, *which*-clauses are always set off by commas.

A compelling reason to use commas to set off clauses beginning with *which* is that failing to do so can result in ambiguity. The reader might be unable to tell whether the writer meant the clause to be defining or nondefining. A fascinating anecdote from the 1984 Republican convention illustrates the point. The story was told by William Safire, a columnist of *The New York Times.*

The platform-writing committee, Mr. Safire said, was divided over the wording of a proposed tax plank. The "pragmatists," led by Senator Robert Dole, wanted the party to appear to be against tax increases without committing itself *never* to raise taxes. The more conservative of the Republican faithful wanted the anti-tax plank to be unequivocal.

The pragmatists came up with,

> We therefore oppose any attempt to increase taxes which would harm the recovery.

The use of *which* without a comma following *taxes* made the sentence confusing — purposely, one might assume. Was the clause, *which would harm the recovery,* defining or nondefining? Did the sentence mean the Republican party was opposed to *any* attempt to increase *any* taxes, or only those taxes that would harm the recovery? If the pragmatists had used *that* rather than *which,* the meaning would have been unmistakable.

But the conservatives knew their grammar. They insisted on inserting a comma in front of *which,* giving the sentence a clear meaning but a different one from what their pragmatic friends intended. One of the pragmatists threatened to "take that comma to the convention floor." But cooler heads prevailed and the conservatives won the day. I feel compelled to point out that we had a tax increase anyway.

My advice about using *which* to introduce a defining clause: Don't.

ABOUT POSSESSIVES

The rule for forming the possessive of a noun is simple: Add an apostrophe and an *s* if the noun is singular. Add only an apostrophe if it is plural. But . . .

But complications arise when a singular word ends in a sibilant, which is a sort of hissing sound (*s, z, c,* or *x*). Some publications have adopted the practice of adding only the apostrophe to such words. For example, the possessive of *boss*, according to that practice, is *boss'*. This results in such sentences as **He married the *boss'* daughter,** which is offensive to my ear and incorrect according to most grammarians. Publications that have adopted that style insist that possessives of such proper names as Gomez and Lomax be formed in the same way. Thus the possessive of Gomez is *Gomez'* and the possessive of Lomax comes out *Lomax'*.

According to the rule cited at the beginning of this discussion, possessives of those three words should be *boss's, Gomez's, and Lomax's.* In all three, the final *s* is pronounced. Therefore, logic is on the side of the rule.

Some exceptions are allowed by authorities who accept the rule. Strunk, for example, suggests adding the apostrophe without the *s* to form the possessives of ancient proper names such as *Moses* and *Achilles. The New York Times Stylebook* permits dropping the final *s* when including it would result in two or more sibilants' preceding the apostrophe, as in **Kansas' governor,** or when a word beginning with a sibilant follows, as in **for appearance' sake.** The stylebook of United Press International instructs UPI editors not to use the apostrophe and the *s* with words of more than one syllable unless the final *s* would be pronounced.

My opinion is that pronunciation is the key. I follow the standard rule for using the apostrophe and the *s* to form the possessive of a singular noun, deviating from it only when adding an *s* would create a word that would require an unnatural pronunciation. Thus, I consider the following possessives of singular nouns to be correct: *Charles's, Jones's, Butz's, Equifax's, Moses',* and *goodness'.* The last two are examples of deviations. *Moses's* and *goodness's* are almost impossible to pronounce.

The preposition *of* provides an alternate way to form a possessive. For example, *the patient's condition* can be expressed as *the condition of the patient.* This form of the possessive can help prevent awkward expressions. Instead of **the President of the United States' office,** most writers would prefer **the office of the President of the United States.** The use of *of* to form possessives sometimes results in a double genitive, as in **a friend of John's.** Although double genitives seem illogical, they are idiomatic English. Rely on your ear.

Note that possessive pronouns (*his, hers, theirs, yours, ours, its, whose*) do not require the apostrophe. Please, please do not use *it's* as a possessive. *It's* means *it is.*

IF THIS WERE SUBJUNCTIVE

In grammar, the subjunctive mood (or mode) is a verb form used to express a condition that is untrue or impossible, or to describe something that could happen but might not. The following contain subjunctive verb forms: **If I were President of the United States; The president requested that Mr. Jones come to his office at once;** and **I would go to the ball game today if I had a ticket.** Note that in each example, the verb form is unusual. *I* does not usually take the verb *were.* Mr. *Jones,* a singular subject, does not usually take the plural verb form, *come.* None of the examples is past tense; all are subjunctive. (Note: *Would go* is a verb phrase used most often to express the simple past tense, as in **When I was a young man, I would go to ball games two or three times a week.**)

In most instances, your ear will tell you when a subjunctive verb is required, but the ear may not be reliable when an "*if*-clause" is involved. The most common misuse of the subjunctive results from the misconception that an *if*-clause is always followed by the subjunctive verb *were.* **If I were you** is an impossible condition; therefore the verb is subjunctive. **If the car was in the garage, he was probably at home** is not a statement contrary to fact, so the correct verb form is the past indicative *was,* not the subjunctive *were.* Ironically, an educated person would be the one most likely to say, **If the car were in the garage** . . . A less educated person probably would say, **If the car was in the garage** . . . In that instance, the less educated person would be right.

Grammarians have been saying goodbye to the subjunctive for

a long time, but, like *whom*, it lives, probably because educated people keep it alive, even if they do misuse it sometimes.

My advice about using the subjunctive: Learn to use it according to current conventions. Disregard it when it seems to make your writing sound unnatural.

SHALL WE USE SHALL?

Excepting questions such as **What shall we do** or **Shall we have dinner now,** *shall* has all but disappeared from American English. *Shall,* in its traditional uses, sounds affected, almost prissy, to the American ear. *Will* and *would* have replaced *shall* and *should* in most uses. My unsupported opinion is that *shall* has faded because distinctions between *shall* and *will* are just too complicated to bother with. Follett devotes twenty-four pages of *Modern American Usage* to *shall, will, should,* and *would.* On the first of those pages he points out that a "historical survey" of those four words consumes one hundred and seventeen pages in Otto Jesperson's *A Modern English Grammar of Historical Principles.*

In legal documents, *shall* is used to express a mandate. For example, **The seller shall deliver a clear title to the property at the time of the closing,** means, in effect, that the seller is required to deliver a clear title. In ordinary (nonlegal) speech or writing, **The seller will deliver a clear title** is a simple statement of what is expected to happen. A mandate would be expressed as **The seller must deliver a clear title.**

Some writers, in a misguided effort to give their writing a legal flavor, will toss in a few *shalls.* It sounds phony; it is phony. My suggestion is, leave *shall* to the lawyers. Shall we move on to Chapter 8?

8.
Know
the Difference

A burro is an ass. A burrow is a hole in the ground. As a [writer] you are expected to know the difference.
— United Press International Stylebook

Writing is, above all, a craft. And a craftsman is one who knows how to use the tools of his craft to create something worthwhile from raw material. Ideas and information are the writer's raw materials. Words are his tools. Using words well means using them with as much precision as possible. In *The Reader Over Your Shoulder*, Robert Graves and Alan Hodge wrote:

No writer of English can be sure of using exactly the right words even in a simple context, and even after twenty or thirty years of self-education. But he should at least act on the assumption that there is always an exactly right word, or combination of words, for his purpose — which he will gratefully recognize as such if it happens to occur to him; and that, though he may not always find the right word, he can at least learn by experience to avoid the quite wrong, and even the not quite wrong ones.

Avoiding the "quite wrong" words is what this chapter is about.

Chapter 3 touched briefly on word usage. This chapter continues that discussion by providing a sort of lexicon of words that are often used incorrectly. It is not intended to replace a good usage manual, which every writer should own and keep handy. It is simply a quick-reference guide to some troublesome words. The ones that seem to me to be the most troublesome have an asterisk (*) beside them. The discussions are not meant to include every possible meaning of a word. Instead, they concentrate on the meanings in which misuse is most common.

adopt/adapt/adept — Both *adopt* and *adapt* are verbs. To *adopt* is to take something as your own. To *adapt* something is to change it. Examples: **The company adopted a new approach to the problem and adapted its organizational structure accordingly; Margaret adopted Sue's recipe, but she adapted it for her taste.** *Adept* is an adjective meaning proficient. Example: **This book will help you become adept at writing clearly and correctly.**

At one time the Japanese were said to follow the practice of adopting the technology of other nations, adapting it for their own purposes, and becoming more adept at it than its originator. Today, however, the Japanese are adept at developing their own.

advise/inform — In business writing, *advise* is overused in the sense of *inform,* as in **Please advise the personnel department of the current status of the employee.** That usage is questionable. Use *advise* when you mean *to give advice* and *inform* when you mean *to give information.*

*affect/effect — *Affect* is a verb; *effect* is usually a noun. Example: **The economic slowdown will affect the company's profit, but the effect likely will be short-lived.** *Effect* can also be a verb meaning to put into effect. Example: **The company will effect a new organizational structure this year.**

aggravate/irritate/exacerbate — *Aggravate* and *irritate* differ in meaning and ought not to be used interchangeably. *Aggravate* means to make worse, as in **The company's problems were aggravated by economic conditions.** *Irritate* means to make angry or impatient, as in **I was irritated by the delay in receiving the check.** Only an existing condition can be aggravated, but irritation is a new condition. Thus, **I was irritated by the delay in receiving the check, and the fact that it was not the correct amount aggravated the situation.** If you're looking for a milder word than *irritate,* try *annoy.*

Exacerbate also means to make worse. It can be used as a synonym for *aggravate.*

alright/all right — Using *alright* for *all right* may be all right with some writers, but not with a writer who writes right. There is no such word as *alright* just as there is no such word as *alwrong*.

alter/altar — *Alter* is a verb meaning to change. An *altar* is a structure, a mound, or a platform where ceremonies, such as weddings, take place. **After you have been led to the altar, you life is altered forever.**

***anxious/eager** — *Anxious* means worried; it is an unpleasant sensation. *Eager* means desirous; it is usually pleasant. **I am eager to finish this book but I am anxious about whether anyone will read it.**

***affluent/effluent** — These two words have a common ancestor, but their meanings are very different. *Affluent* is an adjective meaning prosperous; *effluent* is a noun referring to something that flows out, such as a stream. Most often, it refers to wastes discharged from a manufacturing plant or a sewage-treatment facility. Examples: **Americans today are more affluent than ever; The river was polluted by effluent from a nearby chemical plant.**

apparent/evident — The difference between *apparent* and *evident* is slight, but it's worth knowing. **The man apparently had been drinking** would be appropriate if the man was seen staggering. **The man evidently had been drinking** would be appropriate if some tangible evidence was found, such as empty beer cans on the car seat beside him.

Sometimes one or the other of those words is used when some other word would express the thought more precisely. For example, if the evidence was especially strong, **It was obvious that the man had been drinking** might be better.

***appraise/apprise** — Sentences like **Please keep me appraised of your progress in the matter** are common in business writing. That use of *appraise* is incorrect. *Appraise* means to evaluate. **Please keep me evaluated of your progress** makes no sense. The correct word is *apprised,* which means informed. **I will apprise you of my progress so that you can appraise the situation properly** illustrates correct use of both words. *Inform* is a perfectly good word that is never misunderstood. I prefer it to *apprise*.

***as/like** — Twenty-five or thirty years ago, a cigarette company raised the hackles of grammarians everywhere by adopting the slogan, "Winston tastes good, like a cigarette should." What the grammarians objected to was the use of *like* as a conjunction. Their version of the slogan would have been, "Winston tastes good, *as* a cigarette should."

My feeling was, and is, if that's the most egregious grammatical misstep the advertising industry is ever guilty of, the purity of our language is safe for a millennium. Nevertheless, those who argue for the "purist" use of *like* and *as* have a point or two in their favor. *As*, in this context, means "in the manner of" or "in the way that." The preferred use of *like* is to mean "similar to." Viewed in that way, the grammarians' version of the Winston slogan makes sense. Even so, *like* has been used to mean "in the manner of" for a long time. In spoken English today, it is used as a conjunction more often than *as*. That usage is becoming more common in written English.

In many instances, the idiomatic choice is *like*. The title of a book cited earlier is *Write Like the Pros*. **That smells like bacon cooking** is an acceptable idiom. Theodore Bernstein used the following example in *The Careful Writer:*

> A crowd of young adults raced up and down a Bronx street yesterday carrying marbles in spoons, jumping in potato sacks, and generally behaving as children.

As Bernstein points out, *as* is improper in that sentence. And, as he wryly observes, "it sounds as hell."

One of the worst and most common misuses of *like* is in comparing things that cannot logically be compared. For example, **Like the United States, English is the prevalent language in Great Britain.** Clearly, the United States cannot be compared with English. The sentence should say, **As in the United States, English is the prevalent language in Great Britain.**

Like should not be used in place of *as if*. He walked into the office like he owned it is not an acceptable construction. (See such as/like.)

*average/mean/median — These three words often are used carelessly. Their meanings are quite different. *Average* is determined by adding a series of quantities and dividing by the number of quantities. Thus the average of 10, 25, 100, 80, and 70 is 57 (285 divided by 5).

Mean is the halfway point between two extremes. Thus, if the weather reporter says the high temperature of the month was 60 degrees and the low was 20, the mean temperature of the month was 40, which is halfway between the two extremes. To calculate the mean, simply subtract the lower extreme from the higher, divide the result by 2, and add the result of the division to the lower number (or subtract it from the higher). For example, the mean of 200 and 700 is 450 (700 – 200 = 500; 500 divided by 2 = 250; 250 + 200 = 450; or 700 – 250 = 450).

Median is the tricky one, the one some people assume is the same as *average*. *Median* is the middle number of a series of numbers. Stated another way, half the numbers in a series are above the median, half below. In the 7-number series of 10, 37, 43, 60, 150, 161, and 250, the median is 60. To determine the median of a series with an even number of numbers, add the *two* middle numbers and divide by two. Thus, in the 8-number series of 2, 4, 7, 10, 18, 30, 46, and 110, the median is 14 (10 + 18 = 28, divided by 2 = 14).

Average is also used as a synonym for *typical,* but that usage is proper only when the subject is something that can be measured. Although everyone knows that Yogi is smarter than the average bear, no one has yet figured out exactly what an average bear is. Nor has anyone figured out what an average man is. Unless you're referring to a mathematical average, *typical* almost always is the better choice.

averse/adverse — Both of these closely related words are adjectives, but they have different uses. *Averse* means opposed or antagonistic. It is properly used only to describe a person's attitude. Examples: **The President was not averse to suggestions that he veto the legislation; A stingy person is averse to spending money.** *Adverse* means unfavorable. It almost always describes something inanimate — a circumstance, a force, a condition. Examples: **One of the provisions of the contract was adverse to the company's interests; Low temperatures have an adverse effect on many flowers.** The common error is to use *adverse* when *averse* is indicated. Sentences like **The mayor was adverse to approving an increase in taxes** are considered acceptable — barely — by some authorities. Most, however, consider *adverse* as a synonym for *opposed* to be loose or incorrect usage.

These two words, incidentally, have special meanings in botany. Their meanings are opposite in the sense that they describe opposite directions of growth.

*bad/badly — *Bad* can be a noun, as in *The Good, the Bad, and the Ugly*. But it is usually an adjective. It is used to describe a place, a thing, or a person ("Bad, Bad Leroy Brown"). *Badly* is always an adverb. It is used to qualify a verb by telling how, when or where. That's straightforward enough — except in sentences like **Lydia felt bad this morning, but she came to the office anyway.** Many writers mistakenly believe that an adverb is required in that sentence, and therefore they choose *badly* rather than *bad*. If they do, they're writing badly; or, at least, they're using bad grammar.

Bad, in the example, describes Lydia's condition, not the way in which she goes about the act of feeling. If she were a physician who felt a patient's arm and failed to detect a fracture, you might say she felt *badly.* The principle also applies to *smell.* If you smell *bad,* try a deodorant. If you smell *badly,* go to a physician and have your olfactory nerve tested.

believe/think — I would not get too exercised over the difference between *believe* and *think.* If you want to make a distinction, to *believe* is to have faith; to *think* is to engage in an intellectual process. Personally, I don't *believe* the difference is worth the bother. I don't *think* so, either.

between/among — Most of us were taught that *between* is used when only two things are involved and that *among* is used with three or more. That's still a good rule, but exceptions are not hard to find. If several entities are involved and you want to stress the individuality of each, *between* is proper. Example: **An agreement between the United States, France, Great Britain, and Canada will be consummated this year.** But when you want to emphasize the group, *among* is better. Thus, **Among the four of us, we have $100,000 to invest in the project.**

bring/take — Thoughtlessness rather than ignorance is the most common reason that either *bring* or *take* is used when the other is called for. Both words refer to the act of transporting something from one place to another. The correct choice depends on whether the writer wants to emphasize the origin or the destination. *Take* emphasizes the origin; *bring* emphasizes the destination. Examples: **I often take a bottle of wine to my host when I go to someone's house for dinner, but when I invite guests, I prefer that they do not bring wine; When I leave my office each day, I take my briefcase with me; My wife always brings work home.** The choice between *take* and *bring* in those examples depends on the location of the writer.

*burglar/robber — Burglars often are robbers, but not all robbers are burglars. A *burglar* is someone who breaks and enters with intent to commit a crime, usually theft. A *robber* does his nefarious deed at the point of a gun or other weapon or by intimidation. A *burglar* might break into your home while you're away and haul off your silverware. A robber will put a gun to your back and demand your wallet. Given a choice, I'd take the burglar.

can/may — *Can* denotes the ability to do something. *May* denotes permission. Most of us learned that in grammar school when we asked the teacher, "Can I be excused?" If she was young and inexperienced, she answered, "Yes, you **may.**" If she was wise in the ways of ten-year-old kids, she answered, "No you **may not** until recess." Somehow, I always managed to wait.

*capitol/capital — The *capitol* is the building in which legislatures do their dirty work. The *capital* is the city in which the *capitol* is located. *Capitol building* and *capital city* are redundancies.

Capital is also a financial term used in several senses as a noun or an adjective. **The company is selling bonds to raise capital for expansion; The project will require a large capital investment.**

career/careen — *Career* is most often used to refer to one's profession. But it also means to travel forward at high speed, as in **The motorcycled careered down the highway.** When I was younger I tried using the word in that way a few times, but most readers thought it was a typo, and typesetters always wanted to change it to *careen*, which doesn't mean the same thing at all. *Careen* means to list or tip to one side. **The car careened around the corner** evokes an image of a car rounding a corner on two wheels. Today *careen* is used more often to describe what *career* is supposed to describe. We purists are losing that battle.

casual/causal — What a difference a transposed letter can ·

make! *Casual* means relaxed, informal; *causal* is the adjective form of *cause.* Example: **Bacteria have a causal relation to disease.** Helpful typesetters can't seem to resist changing that sentence to **Bacteria have a casual relation to disease.** That kind of help I can do without.

*****cheap/inexpensive** — The question here is one of connotation. *Cheap* connotes shoddy. *Inexpensive* hints of good sense. I wouldn't want to wear *cheap* clothes, but I'd be delighted to wear inexpensive ones — if I could find any. *Cheap price* is a common redundancy.

*****compare to/compare with** — Experts differ on how to determine when *compare to* is preferable to *compare with.* Their explanations, however, seem to come down to a fairly simple concept: *Compare to* is used with things of different categories, as in the lovely opening line of Shakespeare's Sonnet XVII, "Shall I compare thee to a summer's day?" *Compare with* is used when things of the same category are being discussed. Example: **Net income after taxes was $2.8 million in the fourth quarter, compared with $2.4 million in the fourth quarter of last year.**

*****complement/compliment** — These sound-alikes and almost-look-alikes are far from similar in meaning. As a verb, *complement* means to complete, to supplement, or to supply something that is lacking. Example: **I need a new tie to complement my outfit.** As a noun it means something that complements. It can also mean a complete group. Example: **The ship's complement turned out for the ceremony.** *Full complement* is redundant. *Complement,* whether it's a verb or a noun, always connotes completeness. *Complementary* is the adjective form.

Compliment, as a noun, is an expression of praise. As a verb it means to give a compliment. The adjective form is complimentary. Misuses of *complement* and *compliment* are common, even in the work of people who ought to know better.

*****comprise/compose** — These two words probably are misused as often as any in the language. I rarely use *comprise,* and when I do I usually check the dictionary to be certain I'm using it correctly. *Comprise* means to include or to consist of. Therefore, the whole comprises the parts. Examples: **The English alphabet comprises 26 letters; The company comprises three divisions.** *Compose* means to make up or to put together. The parts compose the whole. Thus, **Twenty-six letters compose the English alphabet; Three divisions compose the company.**

The choice between *comprise* and *compose* depends on what you want to emphasize. *Compose* is the more common. *Is composed of* substitutes nicely for *comprises*. Thus, **The English alphabet is composed of 26 letters; The company is composed of three divisions.** *Comprised of* is never correct.

consensus of opinion/consensus — *Consensus* means agreement, but not necessarily unanimous agreement. *Consensus of opinion* is a redundancy. So is *general consensus*. Neither should be used. *Consensus* is sufficient. *Consensus* is often misspelled "concensus." The reason for the frequent misspelling evidently is the incorrect association of *consensus* with *census*. If you think of *consensus* as being related to *sense*, you probably will have no trouble spelling the word right.

continual/continuous — These words are not synonymous. *Continual* means persistent, or repetitious. *Continuous* means unbroken. Examples: **The continual passing of automobiles disrupted the quiet neighborhood; The north side of the building is a continuous expanse of concrete.** Note that *continual* requires intervals of rest, regardless of how small.

*could care less/couldn't care less — A writer who uses *could care less* is careless and can't even be trusted to learn the correct use of a cliché. I'm not sure why some people want to use *could* when they clearly mean *couldn't*. *Couldn't care less* is the correct choice. The language would not be poorer without either of these expressions.

convince/persuade — The difference here is subtle. To *convince* someone is to win him or her over to your opinion. To *persuade* someone is to get that person to *do* something. Examples: **She convinced me that I needed professional help; She persuaded me to attend a writing seminar.** If this doesn't convince you that these two words differ, that doesn't mean you need professional help.

*criteria/criterion — *Criteria* is the aggrieved party in a hotly contested divorce action. It is trying for a divorce from its singular, *criterion*, just as the plural *data* has become divorced from its singular, *datum.* Unlike *data,* however, *criteria* has not even won a trial separation. (See **data is/data are.**)

Criteria is always plural: **What are the three most important criteria of good writing?** *Criterion* is always singular: **What is the most important criterion of good writing?**

The same holds for *phenomena* (plural) and *phenomenon* (singular). Agenda, however, has been divorced from agendum for a long time and is used as singular in all but the most pedantic writing. *Forum* also is a swinging single, but in that divorce, it was the plural, *fora,* that was kicked out from hearth and home.

data is/data are — Is *data* singular or plural? Yes. That is, it's singular *or* plural, depending partly on your preference, partly on what you want to say. Technically, *data* is plural. Its singular is *datum,* but *datum* is rare except in scientific or academic writing. In other types of writing it is considered by many people to be pretentious. So, if we insist that *data* is plural, what we have is a word that, in effect, has no singular.

Writers disagree on whether *data* can be used as singular. Some always use it as singular; others always use it as plural. Still others let the desired sense determine the choice. Count me among the latter group. If I'm thinking of *data* as a synonym for *information* — a collection of facts — I treat it as singular. If I want to emphasize the individual elements of the collection, I treat the word as plural. Examples: **There is sufficient data** (information) **to support the conclusion; These data** (items of information) **seem to lead to a different conclusion than others we have examined.**

discrete/discreet — *Discrete* means separate; *discreet* means prudent. Examples: **The presentation was made in three discrete parts; The chief executive is very discreet in discussing company business.**

different from/different than — Between *different from* and *different than,* the correct choice usually is *different from.* The reason is, *different* derives from *differ,* a verb that often is followed by the preposition *from.* Thus, **This book is different than other books on writing** is no more correct than **This book differs than others books on writing.** *From* would be correct in both sentences.

Different than is correct when followed by a clause. Example:

His explanation is different than it was last week. To use *from* in that context, you would have to write something like **His explanation is different from the explanation he gave us last week.**

Your ear will be a reliable guide if you follow this suggestion: Always try *different from* in your sentence first. If it sounds right, it probably is. If it doesn't sound right, try *different than.*

*disinterested/uninterested — A *disinterested* person is a person who is impartial or neutral. An *uninterested* person is one who is indifferent. When a person is asked to arbitrate in a dispute between two others, the arbiter is usually a *disinterested* person, but he or she is certainly not *uninterested.* An *uninterested* person is probably bored by the whole thing and would rather be watching a rerun of "I Love Lucy."

*emigrate/immigrate — This depends on whether the subject is coming or going. If a Jew wants to leave the Soviet Union to live in Israel, he wants to *emigrate.* But once he becomes a resident of Israel — if he does — he might hope that some of the friends he left in the workers' paradise will *immigrate* to Israel. If I've made this too complicated, just remember that you *emigrate* from a country, but you *immigrate* to a country. One who emigrates is a emigrant or an émigré; one who immigrates is an immigrant.

eminent/imminent — *Eminent* means prominent, noteworthy, outstanding, celebrated, illustrious, distinguished. Example: **Stephen Hawking is perhaps the most eminent physicist of our time.** *Imminent* means near or impending. Example: **In 1941, America's entry into the war seemed imminent.** In law, the power of the government to appropriate private property for a public purpose is called *eminent domain.* If the government abuses that power, destruction of our freedom may be *imminent.*

enormity/enormousness — Both of these relate to size, but *enormity* is used almost exclusively to describe something evil, appalling, or unthinkable. *Monstrousness* is a synonym. Example: **The jury was outraged by the enormity of the crime.** *Enormousness* may refer to physical size or to size in the figurative sense. In neither reference is it pejorative. Examples: **We were awed by the enormousness of the Sphinx; The enormousness of the good being done by the organization is**

inspiring. *Enormity* would not be correct in either.

*ensure/insure/assure — These words are closely related, but good usage requires recognition that each has a different function. *Ensure* means to make certain, as in **Hard work will almost always ensure success.** *Insure* means, usually, to provide some kind of protection from financial loss, as in **State Farm will insure homes as well as automobiles.** *Assure* means to give comfort or express certainty, as in **I assure you the work will be done on schedule and within budget.**

feasible/possible — A plan or an undertaking can be *possible*, but if high costs or other problems make it impractical, it is not *feasible*. Example: **The engineering department's evaluation of the site determined that building a plant there would not be feasible, although it would be possible given sufficient budget to do the necessary site preparation.**

*fever/temperature — Everyone has a *temperature* all the time. It may be 98.6 or it may be higher or lower. If it's higher, the person has a *fever*. To say a person has a *temperature* when you mean a person has a *fever* is to engage in loose usage.

*few/less — *Few* (or *fewer*) is used to refer to a quantity that usually is expressed by a number; *less* is used with quantities usually expressed in terms other than numbers. Thus, **fewer dollars = less money; fewer hogs = less pork; fewer people = less population.** I doubt that anyone uses *few* where *less* is required, but plenty of people use *less* where *few* is required. **Less dollars, less hogs, less people,** and the like are linguistic barbarisms. In a sentence like We have lived in this house less than ten years, *less* is preferable to *fewer* because we are thinking of ten years as a continuous period rather than ten individual years.

Fewer is the comparative of *few* (*few, fewer, fewest*). The comparative of *less* is *less*, often preceded for emphasis by *still* or *even.* (*less, still less, least*) Lesser is rarely used as a comparative of *less* except in such expressions as "the lesser of two evils."

*flaunt/flout — To *flaunt* is to show off. It often implies ostentation. To *flout* is to ignore or to treat contemptuously. Examples: **Some people can't resist flaunting their wealth; Exceeding**

the speed limit is flouting the law; Anyone who flouts the principles of clear writing flaunts his ignorance.

*forego/forgo — *Forego* is a word you'll probably see used wrong more often than right. It means to go before, but it is often confused with *forgo*, which means to give up or do without. Example: **He decided to forgo the opportunity to buy additional stock in the company.** I'm hard-pressed to come up with an example of a sentence using *forego.* Its past participle, *foregone,* is used often in the slightly shopworn expression *foregone conclusion.* Its present participle, *foregoing,* is also common.

*further/farther — Two asterisks here would not be overstating the case. *Further* is the one more often misused, as in **The intersection is five miles further.** The rule is, use *farther* to indicate distance; use *further* to refer to time, to a continuation, or to an additional quantity of something other than distance. These examples illustrate correct use of both words: **Parts of Nevada are farther west than parts of California; The president requested further information on the matter; Further into the book, the writing grew dull; He would go no further with the discussion.**

founder/flounder — *Founder* means to sink or to fall. It is used most often to refer to a ship, as in **The ship foundered during a storm.** It can, however, refer to a building, an animal, or even a person. *Flounder* means to struggle or to thrash about in disarray. Example: **Witnesses said the man floundered in the water for three or four minutes before disappearing.** *Flounder* can provide good imagery when it's used figuratively, as in **The company floundered for nearly two years before it declared bankruptcy. Sometimes a company flounders and then founders.**

historic/historical — The distinction here is fine but worth making. *Historic* should be reserved for places, things, and events of great significance. Examples: **The Old North Church is one of the nation's most popular historic attractions; President Reagan's nomination of Sandra Day O'Connor to the Supreme Court was an event of historic importance; The Magna Carta is perhaps the world's most precious historic document.** *Historical* refers to history, often in the sense of a particular period of history, or to history as a subject. Example:

Artifacts from the Civil War are of historical significance, but they have little monetary value.

Use the article *a* rather than *an* with both *historic* and *historical.*

if/whether — I am one of a dwindling number of writers who have a strong prejudice against using *if* to introduce a clause, as in **My wife asked me if I would be home for dinner.** I prefer *whether* in such sentences. The reason is that I think of *if* as meaning *in the event that.* Bernstein seems to share my prejudice. He calls *whether* the "normal" word to introduce a noun clause, but he points out that *if* has been so used for centuries. The possibility of ambiguity exists with *if,* but not with *whether.* **My wife asked me to let her know if I would be home for dinner** could mean either my wife wanted me to let her know in the event that I decided to come home for dinner or my wife wanted me to inform her of my decision about coming home for dinner. **My wife asked me to let her know whether I would be home for dinner** has no hint of ambiguity.

I'll continue to prefer *whether* in such sentences, but I doubt that I'll convert many heathens. When you do use *whether,* don't tack on *or not,* a useless appendage most of the time.

*imply/infer — The difference between *imply* and *infer* is not difficult to grasp, but even some good writers fail to grasp it. *Imply* is rarely misused, but *infer* is often used when *imply* is meant. *Infer* means to draw a conclusion on the basis of what you hear, read, or see; *imply* means to convey an impression as opposed to making a clear statement. You cannot *infer* anything by speaking or writing. You can *infer* only by listening, reading, or watching. These examples should make the distinction clear: **The president implied in his speech that he would seek reelection; I inferred from the president's remarks that he would seek reelection; The implication of the president's remarks was that he intended to seek reelection; The inference that could be drawn from the president's speech was that he would seek reelection.**

important/importantly — In a sentence like **The company's sales grew 10 percent last year; more important, earnings grew even more,** many writers would use *importantly* rather than *important.* This is the grammatical twilight zone, but I choose *important* for two reasons: First, *importantly* is an adverb, and I see no logical way it could modify a verb in that sentence; second, *importantly* seems pretentious, although I'm not certain why. *More important* can be considered an ellipsis that means *what's more important.* In fact, a sensible solution to the problem would be to write it that way and thus avoid having to make the choice between *important* and *importantly.*

in behalf of/on behalf of — To speak *in behalf of* someone is to plead that person's case, as in **My colleague said some things to the boss in my behalf.** To speak *on behalf of* someone is to speak in that person's stead, as in **The president of the company spoke on behalf of the chairman, who was unable to attend the meeting.**

liable/likely — The use of *liable* to express either possibility or likelihood, as in **If you play with fire you are liable to be burned** is a mistake. To be *liable* is to incur a liability, usually a legal liability. Example: **If someone slips on the ice on your driveway, he is likely to sue and you may be liable for damages.**

lie/lay — *Lie* is an intransitive verb, which means it does not take an object. *Lay* is transitive. Examples: **I sometimes lie down for a nap on Sunday afternoon; I will lay down the book after I have finished this chapter.** The main reason for confusion is that *lay* is also the past tense of *lie.* Then we have the past participles to contend with. Lain is the past participle of *lie.* (**I have lain here all afternoon.**) *Laid* is the past participle of *lay* (**I have laid the matter to rest.**)

English is one more confusing language. And that's no lie.

like/such as — I'm reluctant to tackle this one. Writers whom I respect disagree on whether there is any significant difference between *like* and *such as.* Wilson Follett and Theodore Bernstein say no. James J. Kilpatrick says yes. I come down — gingerly — on the side of Kilpatrick. His argument seems valid: "When we are talking of large, indefinite fields of similarity, *like* properly may be used . . . When we are talking about specifically named persons [places or things] . . . included in a small field, we ought to use *such as.*"

In **Books like this one can help you write better,** *like* means similar to. In **Cities such as Atlanta and Birmingham are**

important to the economy of the Southeast, the intent is to specify those cities as examples, not merely to put them into a broad category of cities that are important to the economy of the Southeast.

majority/plurality — *Majority* is any amount more than fifty percent. *Plurality* is the highest of three or more numbers when none is a *majority*. If a candidate wins an election with forty percent of the votes cast, he has won with a plurality of forty percent. In using *plurality* it is necessary to specify what the total consists of. For example, the number of votes a candidate receives can be a *majority* of the votes cast yet only a *plurality* of eligible voters. In this sense, many elections in the United States are decided by pluralities. Sad.

may/might — Grammatically, there is no difference between *may* and *might* when they're used to express uncertainty. Most of the time the two are interchangeable. To the sensitive ear, however, *might* connotes a slightly greater degree of uncertainty. Example: **If you read this book, you may learn to write better, and you might even earn more money.** In speech, *might* may be emphasized slightly to show greater doubt.

Technical differences in *may* and *might* relate to tense, but they are not troublesome enough to discuss here.

mobile/movable — Promoters of the mobile-homes industry like to say that most mobile homes stay put. No doubt that's true. But it is also true that mobile homes can be moved. That makes them *movable*. Something (or someone) that can move (as opposed to can be moved) is properly referred to as *mobile*. A person may be *immobilized* by an injury, even though a doctor may determine that he is *movable*. In that sense, *movable* is figurative rather than literal. It means, of course, that the victim can be moved without endangering his life. *Immovable* usually refers to something in a fixed position — e.g., a tree, a mountain, or a structure.

oral/verbal — *Oral* refers to the mouth. Therefore, *oral* communication is speech. *Verbal* refers to words. Therefore, *verbal* communication is communication that uses words, whether the words are written or spoken. In this sense, the famous line attributed — perhaps erroneously — to the late movie mogul Sam Goldwyn is not so funny after all. Goldwyn is reported to have told an aide, "A verbal contract is not worth the paper it's written on." In common usage, however, *verbal* almost always means *oral.* If someone tells you he has a verbal contract, you can bet he has nothing in writing.

I would prefer that the two words be used as they were intended to be used, but the use of *verbal* as a synonym for *spoken* is ingrained in the language.

over/more than — Most of us have expressions we love to hate. One of mine is *over* as a substitute for *more than,* as in **A good automobile costs over $10,000.** *Over* in that sense is common enough, but I still don't like it. I prefer to reserve *over* for references to location, as in **The airplane flew over Soviet territory.**

pabulum/Pablum — *Pabulum* (not capitalized) is a food that nourishes a plant or an animal. The word is also used figuratively to mean food for intellectual thought. *Pablum* (capitalized) is a trademark for a brand of baby food. Both words are used to describe something that is excessively simple or bland.

Maunufacturers usually cannot register a common word for use as a trademark, so they sometimes work a little creative magic on the spelling and come up with something they can protect. It's probably safe to say that the *Pablum* folks created their trademark by misspelling *pabulum.* Manufacturers don't do the language any favors by engaging in such shenanigans, but they don't mind asking writers to help them protect their trademarks by capitalizing them. As my friends at The Coca-Cola Company might say, "Put a cap on Coke." That is, unless you mean either the fuel or the (barely) controlled substance that comes in through Florida.

*pom pom/pompon — A fancier of World War II movies should know about antiaircraft guns that go pom-pom-pom-pom-pom and make little puffs of black smoke all around enemy planes. That type of gun is a *pom pom* (sometimes written *pompom* or *pom-pom*). A *pompon* is one of those fluffy ornamental balls or tufts often seen on festive costumes.

prescribe/proscribe — If these words confuse you, consult your friendly neighborhood dictionary. *Prescribe* means to direct, to dictate, or to set forth (rules); *proscribe* means to prohibit, condemn, or put aside. The two are almost opposites.

principle/principal — *Principle* is always a noun. It means a fundamental, as in **This book sets forth some of the principles of good writing.** *Principal* can be either a noun or an adjective. As an adjective, it means main or most important, as in **The principal ingredients of salad dressing are oil and vinegar.** As a noun it can refer to a person who is the administrative head of a school, to a partner in a business, to a party in a legal agreement, or to a sum of money.

A grammar school teacher gave me a mnemonic device to help me keep all this straight. "Think of our principal as your PAL," she said, stressing princiPAL. That wasn't easy, but I managed. She also suggested visualizing *principal* as principAl and letting the big A stand for adjective. It worked then. I confess I still use it.

proceed/precede — *Proceed* means to go forward; *precede* means to go before. Because *procedure* is derived from *proceed*, it is sometimes misspelled *proceedure*.

raise/raze — These words are almost opposite in meaning. *Raise* means to lift up; *raze* means to tear down.

*sewage/sewerage — *Sewage* is waste; *sewerage* is the system of pipes that carry the sewage to wherever sewage is carried — not, let us hope, into our rivers and streams. *Sewerage* should not be used as an adjective. To do so is to be redundant. In **The developer installed sewerage lines in the subdivision,** *sewerage lines* is redundant. *Sewage lines,* however, would be acceptable in that sentence, but *sewerage* is the better choice.

site/cite — These sound-alikes are unrelated. *Site* is usually a noun meaning location, as the *site* of a building. It is used sometimes as a verb meaning to place on location, as in **The engineer sited the building well.** *Sited* is a better choice than *situated* in sentences like **The plant was sited on seven acres.**

Cite means to call attention to, as in **The teacher cited three examples of good writing.**

stalactite/stalagmite — If you're a spelunker, you probably know that a *stalactite* is a deposit of calcium carbonate that hangs from the "ceiling" of a cave and a *stalagmite* is a deposit of calcium carbonate that sticks up from the "floor." A good way to keep them apart is to let the *c* in *stalactite* stand for "ceiling."

Forget the one about "stuck tight." Something can be stuck tightly to the floor as easily as to the roof.

*tandem/parallel — Many good writers use *tandem* when they mean *parallel.* When two things are *parallel,* they are side by side. When they are *in tandem,* one follows the other. I often read sentences like **The two projects proceeded in tandem.** Usually the writers of such sentences mean the projects went forward at the same time. If that's what they mean, *in parallel* or *together* would be appropriate, but not *in tandem.* If the writer of that sentence meant *in tandem,* he would have to say which of the two projects went first in order for the sentence to make sense.

this/that — As demonstratives, *this* and *that* are used interchangeably by some writers. They should not be. *This* refers to something close at hand, e.g., **this book I am holding; this idea I am discussing.** *That* refers to something farther away either in distance or in time, e.g., **that book on the shelf; that idea we discussed yesterday.** *These* and *those* are plurals of *this* and *that.*

these (those) kind/this (that) kind — *These kind* and *those kind* are linguistic hybrids that have no place in either writing or speech. *Kind* is singular and therefore takes a singular demonstrative adjective. *This kind, that kind, these kinds,* and *those kinds* are all correct.

transpire/occur — Some dictionaries now list *transpire* as a synonym for *occur.* Many authorities, however, consider that to be loose usage. The traditional meaning of *transpire* is to leak out (as a vapor) and thus become apparent. Used that way, *transpire* strongly connotes the airing of information previously secret. The battle to preserve this traditional and useful meaning is probably lost, but I still would not use *transpire* to mean *occur.* There are better synonyms for *occur* — e.g., *happen, take place.*

turgid/turbid — *Turgid* means swollen; *turbid* means cloudy or muddy. Examples: **The child's belly was turgid from malnutrition; The old man's eyes were turbid as a result of cataracts.**

ultimate/penultimate — *Ultimate* means last; but it often connotes superiority, especially when used by ad copywriters addicted to overstatement. Thus, **The ultimate driving machine**

means the finest automobile, the last word in automobiles. *Penultimate* means next to last. It carries no connotation of quality. It means next to last, period. Example: **The penultimate letter of the alphabet is** *y.*

And this is the penultimate entry in our lexicon of troublesome words and phrases.

while/although — Almost everyone, including me, occasionally uses *while* instead of *although, and,* or *but.* (**While I am not a great golfer, I am an enthusiastic one; I ate a steak, while my wife had only a salad.**) The language would be better off if *while* were restricted to uses related to time, as in **I enjoyed a movie while my wife was shopping.** Bernstein suggests that using *while* instead of *although* is a symptom of "monologophobia," a made-up word to describe the fear of repeating a word. A "monologophobe," he says, is "a writer who would rather walk naked in front of Saks Fifth Avenue than be caught using the same word more than once in three lines."

9.
Uses and Misuses of Punctuation

*Punctuation . . . is one of those devices
invented to translate words from a
natural medium, the spoken language,
to an artificial medium, writing.*
— James C. Raymond, *Writing (Is an Unnatural Act)*

Of all the devices that help make writing "reader-friendly," none is more important than punctuation. Imagine, if you can, how "unfriendly" writing would be with no punctuation at all. Professor Raymond points out that punctuation developed after writing, not along with it as we might suppose. Early writing, he says, had no punctuation, and some early forms of writing went from left to right and from right to left in alternating lines, much as a high-speed printer prints a page. Readers were required not only to supply their own punctuation but also to read backward.

More than anything, punctuation establishes the relationship of the parts of a sentence to the whole of a sentence and to each other. It also helps establish the pace of the writing, and it contributes in no small way to meaning.

Punctuation is for the reader, not the writer. If you have written a passage, it must be assumed that you know what you intended to say even if you did not punctuate well. But your readers have no such advantage. For them, punctuation is what they believe it to be. And that is the basic reason for adopting rules, or conventions, of punctuation — that is, for consistency.

Rules of punctuation are not necessarily logical. They are often arbitrary. Newspapers and magazines emphasize consistency, and most publications mandate certain conventions for their writers and editors to follow. These conventions may vary slightly among publications, and if you write for a particular publication, you should study that publication or obtain a copy of its stylebook.

This chapter discusses the main punctuation marks and their uses. It is designed to be a guide, albeit not a complete guide, for writers who want to punctuate according to generally accepted standards. Books devoted to punctuation are available, but any good dictionary will provide answers to most punctuation questions.

The punctuation marks we will discuss in this chapter are the apostrophe, the colon, the comma, the dash, the ellipsis, the hyphen, parentheses, the period, the question mark, quotation marks, and the semicolon.

APOSTROPHE

The apostrophe has two important uses: (1) To form possessives, and (2) To form contractions or to show the omission of letters or figures.

Using the Apostrophe to Form Possessives

To form the possessive of a singular noun, add an apostrophe and an s. Examples: *the policeman's gun, Charles's hat, the boss's daughter.* Some grammarians and some publications differ on forming the possessive of singular words ending in sibilants. (See Chapter 7 for a discussion of these differences.) Probably the most sensible practice is to add the s after the apostrophe if you would pronounce it.

To form the possessive of plural words that end in s, add only the apostrophe. Examples: *the Joneses' son, the readers' opinions, cities' mayors.* For a plural word that ends in a letter other than s, form the possessive as if the word were singular. Examples: *the people's choice, the men's room.*

Possessive forms of personal pronouns do not require the apostrophe. An exception is *one.* The possessive of *one* is *one's.* The possessive pronouns are *his, hers, yours, theirs, ours, mine, whose,* and *one's.* (Note: *It's* means *it is.* The word is often mistakenly used where the possessive *its* is required.)

When two or more words, taken as a unit, are possessive, use the possessive with the last word only. *Todd and Jim's car* shows joint possession of one car. If two cars are involved, *Todd's and Jim's car* would show individual possession. The expression is elliptical for *Todd's car and Jim's car.*

The apostrophe is optional, but preferred by most writers, in expressions such as *a year's time, a day's pay,* and *two weeks' vacation.*

Using the Apostrophe with Contractions

Common contractions include *I've* (I have), *he's* (he is), *you're* (you are), *they're* (they are), *haven't* (have not), *I'd* (I would), *isn't* (is not). Most contractions are a combination of a verb and either its subject or a negative modifier. The apostrophe is used to show the omission of one or more letters. Contractions with personal pronouns, as in several of the examples above, are natural, but contractions with proper nouns can be awkward. *John's* (John is) *going with us* is acceptable, but most writers would prefer *John is.* Don't try to form other contractions with proper nouns. It doesn't work.

Other Uses of the Apostrophe

The apostrophe is used to show the omission of numbers in such uses as the *fall of '87* and the omission of letters in expressions that attempt to imitate certain speech patterns, such as *finger lickin' good.*

The apostrophe is also used to form plurals of single letters or numbers when they appear in the body of a text. Example: **Mary brought home a report card with three A's and two B's.** The purpose of using the apostrophe in this way is to prevent confusion. Therefore, using the apostrophe to form plurals of groups of letters or numbers is not necessary except when letters are followed by periods. Examples: **the 1920s, the ABCs, the rule of 78s, two Ph.D.'s.**

COLON

Henry Fowler is believed by many to have been the foremost authority on usage. In *Modern English Usage,* Fowler wrote that the colon "has acquired a special function: that of delivering goods that have been invoiced in the preceding words."

What are the "goods" that the colon delivers? They can be a list, a long quotation, or a statement that explains or expands on immediately preceding information.

Use of the colon is often just a stylistic preference: Many writers like to use a colon when a period would serve as well. That sentence, of course, makes its own point. In Fowler's sentence, the colon could not be replaced by a period, but the colon has almost the strength of a period. If the material following the colon expresses a complete thought, begin it with a capital letter.

Colons can be used to introduce long lists of itemized information or short lists within a sentence. Example: **I have three goals in life: to be healthy, to do useful work, and to leave the world better than I found it.**

Use of the colon to introduce a long quotation may be doing the reader a favor because it tells the reader right away who is being quoted; for example: **Wilson Follett had this to say about the colon: "The colon is used to introduce formally. It furnishes this service for lists, tables, and quotation, or for the second member of a two-sentence statement when the first raises an expectation or makes a promise to be fulfilled by the second."**

COMMA

The most important function of a comma is to indicate a natural pause. The writer who uses commas in that way, without bothering consciously to follow rules, will not be wrong often. One problem with that approach, however, is that a pause that is natural to one reader is not necessarily natural to another. The approach tends to result in more commas than modern writers like to use. Although too many commas can be distracting, it seems better, in the interest of clarity, to have too many than too few. Those who argue against relying too much on the ear say that writing is meant to be seen, not heard, and therefore the eye is more reliable. It's probably unwise to take the extreme of either of these positions.

Commas are used by some writers to create certain effects or to emphasize points just as a pause in speaking can be used for emphasis.

Whether you are a "heavy user" or a "light user" of commas, a little time spent in learning the commonly accepted conventions is time spent in the interest of reader-friendly writing. To summarize the most important of these, I have identified four categories of uses of commas: Joining, Inserting, Listing, and Introducing. Note the initial letters of those four categories form a pronounceable acronym, JILI. If you are fond of memory aids, you're welcome to use that one to help you remember the four main uses of commas.

Commas are used in:

Joining two independent clauses to form a compound sentence using *and, or, but, nor, yet, for,* or *so.* An independent clause is a clause that expresses a complete thought and thus could stand alone. **The company lost money last year, but management expects substantial earnings this year** is a compound sentence consisting of two independent clauses. In compound sentences, the comma often is omitted if the two clauses are short and closely related. Usually it is safe to omit the comma when the conjunction is *and* or *or* unless ambiguity would result. Omission of the comma when some other conjunction introduces the second clause is not recommended.

Do not use a comma before *and* or *or* unless the conjunction begins a complete thought. In the sentence **I don't want your money or your sympathy,** *or your sympathy* is not a complete thought; therefore, no comma is required after *money.* If you're trying for a dramatic pause after *money,* a comma isn't strong enough. A dash is better: **I do not want your money — or your sympathy.**

Do *not* use a comma to join an independent clause with a dependent clause. A dependent clause is not a complete thought. Example: **The rules of grammar are important because they lend clarity and order to writing.** *Because they lend clarity and order to writing* is a dependent clause. Changing *because* to *and* would result in two independent clauses, making a comma desirable before *and.*

An important exception to the rule about not using a comma

to join an independent clause and a dependent clause is a *because* clause preceded by a negative statement. In such sentences, a comma may be necessary to prevent ambiguity. (See Chapter 4.)

Inserting nonessential material in a sentence. Nonessential material can be an appositive, a parenthetical expression, a nonrestrictive clause or phrase, or a conjunctive adverb. In the following examples, the italicized words are not essential to the main ideas of the sentences. **The company,** *nevertheless,* **still plans to introduce the product; Mrs. Jones,** *a mother of three,* **works in a department store.** Failure to use commas to set off nonessential material can make the material seem to be essential to the meaning. An illustration of ambiguity caused by the omission of commas appears in Chapter 4 under "Punctuate for Clarity."

Listing words or phrases in a series. Example: **I went to the drug store to buy toothpaste, soap, shaving cream, and razor blades.** Note that I have put a comma before *and,* which precedes the last item in the series. This is called the "serial comma." Most newspapers and many other publications do not advocate using the serial comma. Most grammarians, however, do. Omitting it can result in misunderstanding about what the writer meant to say. Example: **The soldier told me that the things he missed most about home were his dog, his little brother, the odor of his dad's pipe and his girl friend.** My feeling about the serial comma is simple: It can't do any harm, and it might do some good. I recommend it.

Introducing a thought with a phrase or clause. Example: **In the war years of 1941-1944, the United States experienced shortages of many commodities.** When introductory phrases are short, and when no ambiguity would result, the comma can be omitted. Some stylebooks give the maximum number of words an introductory phrase or clause can have if the comma can be omitted. There is no good reason for such an arbitrary rule. Common sense and a good ear are better ways to determine whether a comma would increase clarity. **In 1944 the United States was still experiencing shortages of many commodities** is acceptable without a comma after *In 1944.* A comma there would cause a subtle shift of emphasis, as though the writer intended to contrast the situation of 1944 with that of another year. In sentences like **After the dogs had finished eating the men returned to the house to clean their shotguns,** a comma is needed after *eating* so the reader will not get the idea that the dogs ate the men — unless that's what happened.

Other Uses of Commas

So much for JILI. Here are some additional uses of the common comma:

1. Use commas to separate adjectives in a series if the adjectives are of equal importance. Example: **They live in a large, well-designed, comfortable house.** Another way to look at this is that the commas in that sentence are used instead of *and.* Do not use commas to separate adjectives in a series if the adjectives seem to be so closely related as to almost form a single thought or if inserting *and* between them would seem inappropriate. Example: **They live in a large white two-story house.** The ear is usually reliable in such instances.

2. Use commas to set off contrasting phrases within a sentence. Example: **The man went into the store, not to make a purchase, but to ask directions.**

3. Use a comma or commas to set off a complete quotation. Examples: **He said, "Writing is one of the skills we often find lacking in recent graduates"; "Writing," he said, "is one of the skills we often find lacking in recent graduates."** Partial quotations are not set off by commas. Example: **The personnel director said that writing is "one of the skills we find lacking" in recent graduates.**

4. Use a comma to set off a direct address. Example: **Mister, can you spare two dollars for cup of coffee?**

5. Use a comma to indicate a missing word or words. Example: **Maryjane is 12 years old; Carolyn, [is] 8.**

6. Use a comma whenever one would prevent confusion. Example: **Whatever will be, will be.**

7. Use commas to set off the year from the day of the month. Example: **May 7, 1955 was an important day in my life.** Do not use a comma after the month when the day is not included. Example: **May 1955** (not **May, 1955**).

DASH

The dash is used to interrupt the main thought and introduce supporting or explanatory material. The inserted words are set off by a pair of dashes if they occur in the body of a sentence. A dash indicates an abrupt stop stronger than a comma, but not as strong as a period.

ELLIPSIS

In syntax, an ellipsis is the intentional omission of a word or words. When a portion of a direct quotation is omitted, the ellipsis is indicated by three periods (. . .). This is called an ellipsis mark or, sometimes, ellipsis points. For spacing purposes, an ellipsis mark is treated as a 3-letter word. For example: **"We the people of the United States . . . do ordain and establish this Constitution . . . ."** In this abbreviated quotation from the preamble to our Constitution, words are omitted in two places. Note that I used a space and four dots at the second omission. This is because the omitted material would complete the sentence. The first three dots are the ellipsis points, the fourth is a sentence-ending period. If the complete quote had been a question, I would have used three dots and a question mark (-ion . . .?").

Style manuals differ on ellipsis points. Some simplify the matter by suggesting three dots (. . .) for an omission, no matter where it occurs. Others, especially manuals for preparation of academic manuscripts, have stringent rules.

I suggest you adopt a style that suits you and use it consistently.

EXCLAMATION POINT

The exclamation point (!) is much beloved of high school sophomores. Professional writers don't use it often, because they consider it a substitute — a poor one at that — for a well-chosen word. Never use two exclamation points together.

HYPHEN

The main purpose of the hyphen is to prevent awkward or confusing constructions. Most often, hyphens join two or more words that, taken together, form an adjective. Examples: **busi-**

ness-writing seminar, front-office decision, in-house legal counsel, state-of-the-art equipment. In such examples, the hyphens ensure clarity and make reading easier. Use of hyphens in this way has been hotly debated by writers. Some favor hyphens in all such constructions. Others use hyphens when they are necessary to prevent ambiguity. My inclination is to use hyphens frequently because of my zeal to make my writing as easy to read as possible, but the modern trend is to use fewer hyphens.

Adding to the general confusion surrounding the question is the trend toward combining two words into one compound word, such as *businessman, stockbroker, healthcare,* and *handgun.* Some manuals of style include lists of such words, but you can also find them individually in your dictionary. *Businessman* sometimes causes problems when a modifier is required. For example, *small businessman* leaves doubt as to whether *small* refers to the size of the business or to the size of the man. Assuming the former, it should be written as *small-business man.*

Some additional uses for hyphens are:

1. To avoid awkward double- or triple-letter combinations. Examples: **re-elect, anti-industrial, pre-eminent.**

2. To form compound numbers less than one hundred. Examples: **twenty-one, sixty-seven, ninety-nine, three-sixteenths, one-fourth.**

3. To join a prefix to a proper noun. Examples: **un-American, pre-Christmas, ex-President Carter, anti-Soviet.**

Do not use a hyphen to join a word that ends in *-ly* with another word to form a compound. No hyphens are needed in **publicly held company, wholly owned subsidiary, widely known facts.**

PARENTHESES

There's not much debate about the use of parentheses, but they are often used when commas or dashes would serve as well and would be less distracting. Some manuals say that material in parentheses carries less emphasis than material set off by commas or dashes. I've never quite understood that distinction. One thing is certain: Parentheses must be used when the material to be enclosed is a complete sentence. In that case, the punctuation is within the parentheses.

In my opinion, parentheses should always be in pairs. Some publications use a single parenthesis with numbers or letters marking items in a series. Example: **The plaintiff asked for a) restitution for damages b) attorneys' fees c) written assurance that similar incidents would not occur again.** If there's a reason for not using pairs of parentheses to enclose *a*, *b*, and *c*, I'm not aware of it. The best reason for doing so is that a parenthesis looks lonely by itself.

PERIOD

Other than to mark the end of a sentence, the only function of a period is to show an abbreviation. Periods are *not* used with acronyms — pronounceable abbreviations such as NATO, HUD, and NASA. Many publications omit periods with abbreviations that are well known and usually appear in all capital letters, such as *FBI*, *USA*, and *HEW*, even though they are pronounced one letter at a time. Abbreviations of single words — months, days, titles, etc. — and relatively unfamiliar abbreviations always require periods.

The period has been called the most under-used punctuation mark — a reference to the fact that too-long sentences are a common symptom of bad writing. Both the Fog Index and the Flesch readability measuring system emphasize shorter sentences (See Chapter 5). Writing should not be all short, choppy sentences, but a good piece of advice is, when in doubt, reach for a period instead of a semicolon or conjunction.

QUESTION MARK

When a sentence ends with a quoted question, the question mark is the terminal punctuation, and a period is not needed. Example: **Turning to face the President, the reporter asked, "Mr. President, what is your reaction to the trade bill now being debated in Congress?"**

When a sentence begins with a quoted question, the question mark eliminates the need for a comma to set off the quotation from the attribution. Example: **"What is your opinion of the bill now being debated in Congress?" the reporter asked the President.**

Question marks are used only with direct questions, not when questions are simply referred to. Examples: **In the Watergate hearings, Senator Baker asked the now-famous question, what did the President know and when did he know it; The now-famous question, what did the President know and when did he know it, was asked by Senator Baker in the Watergate hearings.**

QUOTATION MARKS

The main uses of quotation marks are to set off direct quotations, titles of short works, words or phrases used in an unusual way, and nicknames

With direct quotations, confusion persists about the location of punctuation in relation to the quotation marks. The conventions are not all logical, but here they are:

1. Periods and commas always go inside the quotation marks. Examples: **"The company is in good financial shape," he said; He said, "The company is in good financial shape."**

2. Semicolons always go outside the quotation marks. Example: **He said, "The company is in good financial shape"; but then he proceeded to cite figures that led to a different conclusion.**

3. Question marks and exclamation marks go either inside or outside, depending on whether the question or exclamation is part of the quoted material. Examples: **Mr. Jones asked, "What is the source of that information?"; Was it Mr. Jones who asked, "What is the source of that information."?**

4. A quotation within a quotation is set off by single quotation marks. Example: **"One of my favorite lines," he said, is Dylan Thomas's 'Do not go gentle into that good night.'"** Note that the both the single and double quotation marks go after the period.

Short works whose titles are set off by quotation marks include poems, book chapters, magazine articles, songs, and short stories. Longer works, such as motion pictures, books, operas, and concertos, usually appear in italics. Italics are indicated in typewritten copy by underlining.

A word or phrase used in an unusual way is enclosed in quotation marks the first time it is so used. Unless there is a lot of space between the first and subsequent uses, the quotation marks are necessary only once.

SEMICOLON

The semicolon has been described as a punctuation mark that indicates a pause that is stronger than the pause indicated by the comma but weaker than the pause indicated by a period. Actually, a semicolon is much closer to a period than a comma.

The most important function of the semicolon is to join closely related independent clauses. Example: **The company introduced a dozen new products last year; ten were introduced the previous year; and only seven were introduced the year before that.** Independent clauses can be joined by a comma when a conjunction is used, but when independent clauses are joined by *however*, a semicolon must be used instead of a comma. Example: **The company introduced several new products last year; however, unless the economy improves, none will be introduced this year.**

Semicolons are useful in separating phrases in a list when the individual phrases already contain commas. Example: **Present at the meeting were Mr. White, the chief executive officer; Mr. Phillips, the chief financial officer; and Mr. Gray, a representative of the company's public relations agency.**

EXERCISE 12: PUNCTUATION

Test your knowledge of punctuation by correcting the sentences below. Some of them contain unnecessary or incorrect punctuation; others omit punctuation that should be used.

1. Margaret Mitchell, author of "Gone With the Wind," was a native of Georgia; however, she became known throughout the world.

2. The company has offices in Atlanta, Georgia; Tacoma, Washington; Birmingham, Alabama; and San Juan, Puerto Rico.

3. Sally is ten years old; her brother is only three.

4. "The ability to write well," he said, "is one of the most important skills a businessman can have."

5. Before he became president of the company, he was eastern regional manager.

6. Before he became president of the company, he founded another company that manufactured the same products.

7. "Let's eat, Harry; I'm starved," said Bill.

8. What is, is; what will be, will be.

9. The ability to write well, understand complex ideas, think clearly, and speak before a group are attributes that will serve anyone well.

10. "I have nothing to offer but blood, toil, tears, and sweat," said Winston Churchill, the great World War II leader.

11. December 7, 1941, is known as "Pearl Harbor Day." President Roosevelt called it "a day that will live in infamy."

12. The United States declared war on Japan in December, 1941. The declaration of war followed the Japanese attack on Pearl Harbor.

13. After World War II, the United States led the way to the formation of the "North Atlantic Treaty Alliance" (N.A.T.O.), which had as its objective the defense of Europe.

14. As rich as he is, he still goes out of his way to save a penny or two.

15. The group included first, second, and third-grade students.

16. Was it John Kennedy who said, "Ask not what your country can do for you . . .?"?

17. Kennedy made that statement, not on the floor of the Senate, but in his inaugural address.

18. In army slang, a "shavetail" is a second lieutenant. The commanding officer is often referred to as "the old man." I was a

Which: do not have identification in the sentence.
that: have to have info in that. ex. This is the book that I told you about.

either use , ( ) or dash .

22-year-old shavetail and was briefly a company commander. I often wondered whether the men in my company, most of whom were older than I was, called me the old man.

19. The student asked, "Who was it who wrote, all the world's a stage and all the men and women merely players"? ?

20. The company has done very well in the past two years, but this year is going to be a very difficult one.

10.
Some
Closing Thoughts

Remember that what you write may be your
legacy. Give it as much care as you can.
— Ronald L. Goldfarb and James C. Raymond,
Clear Understandings

If I have done what I set out to do in writing this book, and if you have used the book as I suggested, then congratulations to both of us! We have just completed a successful seminar on writing. Usually near the end of one of my seminars I think of things I had meant to cover but didn't, and I'm having the same experience now as I near the end of the book. Therefore, I want to use this, the final chapter, as I often use the last half hour or so of a seminar — to elaborate on some of the points I made earlier and even to introduce some new material.

First, some comments about the importance of revising: In reading the first draft of the book, I found several places where I apparently failed to follow my own advice, which can be embarrassing. I also found some bad writing and questionable punctuation.

Confession time? No, this is just my way to illustrate the point, made by someone whose name I cannot recall, that there is no good writing, only good *rewriting*. To that bit of wisdom I would only add that good editing makes better writing, whether the editor is the writer or someone else.

An analogy that seems so apt, a sentence that's as clear as mountain air, a phrase that you're certain is turned to perfection, a word that expressed your precise meaning — all these may look different on another day or to another pair of eyes.

First-draft writing is rarely good enough for someone who is serious about writing. Anyone who is satisfied with his first draft has either abundant talent or low standards. In most cases, it's probably the latter. Even writers who revise as they go usually do two or three drafts before they have an acceptable piece. The draft of this book that I submitted to my publisher was either the third or fourth, depending on how you would choose to count. Some sections I revised five or six times. Several of my colleagues read all or parts of the book, and of course my publisher's editor had a go at it. All of these people looked at the copy far more objectively than I ever could.

In revising my first draft, I set out to eliminate the truly bad writing and to improve all the writing, good and bad. I compared my punctuation with the conventions in Chapter 9 to make certain there were no inconsistencies. Where I found I had violated some rule or principle, I tried to determine whether I had done so for good reason or whether some bad habit had asserted itself. Not surprisingly, I found the latter to be the case most often. In a few instances, however, I did have a good reason for departing from the principle. My philosophy is that one reason for learning rules is to know when you can break them with impunity. The novelist George Orwell seemed to agree, as evidenced by the sixth of his six elementary rules of good writing, published in 1946:

1. Never use a metaphor, simile or other figure of speech which you are used to seeing in print.

2. Never use a long word when a short one will do.

3. If it is possible to cut out a word, always cut it out.

4. Never use the passive where you can use the active.

5. Never use a foreign phrase, a scientific word or a jargon word if you can think of an everyday English equivalent.

6. Break any of these rules sooner than say anything outright barbarous.

Good advice from a distinguished author: Learn the rules and follow them unless you have good reason not to. I am reasonably certain that on occasion Orwell used longer-than-necessary words, foreign words with English equivalents, and words that could have been omitted. I doubt, however, that he ever said anything outright barbarous. Rules, principles, conventions — whatever you choose to call them — do not make good writing. Nor does violating them always result in bad writing. Rules are guidelines, not substitutes for thought.

GOOD WRITING, CLEAR THINKING

Clear writing is invariably a product of clear thinking. At breakfast one morning recently I found myself reading the back of a cereal box — a lifelong habit. I noticed a "non-word," *naturly*, which I took to be a misspelling of *naturally*. The writer of that copy probably thought he was writing the adverbial form of *nature* rather than *natural*. Of course, if *naturly* had been italicized, cap-italized, or boldfaced, or if some other typographical contrivance had been used, I might have thought the misspelling was just one of the cutesy-cutesy departures from convention that enamor some copy writers. Absent such, I assumed it to be an error. The error would have been prevented by clear thinking on the writer's part. Clear thinking would also prevent errors like the one illus-trated by sentence number two in the second part of Exercise 8, Chapter 4:

> The ability to write well, we believe, is one of the things that (set/ sets) her apart.

The writers who selects *sets* rather than *set* in that example – and many do — simply is not thinking clearly. You don't have to know a rule of grammar to know that *things* cannot be paired with *sets*. Your ear and your common sense tell you that *things that sets her apart* is not good English. Misplaced modifiers, un-clear antecedents, faulty parallelism, and other grammatical or syntactical blemishes that mar our writing would yield to a smidgen of clear thought.

ACHIEVING COHESIVENESS

One of the most common writing problems I see in the work of seminar participants is lack of cohesiveness. They often show me samples of writing that just doesn't "hang together" even though the individual sentences are well-constructed. Writing cohesive sentences is relatively easy. Writing cohesive paragraphs is a little harder, and writing cohesive passages consisting of several paragraphs is harder still. Writing cohesively is easier if the writer understands grammar, punctuation, sentence structure, and transitions; but thoughtful attention to content and sequence is essential.

To write copy that hangs together, you must consider how each element (word, phrase, sentence, paragraph) relates to and affects other elements, especially those that immediately follow and precede it. The objective is to lead the reader smoothly from one sentence to the next and from one paragraph to the next. Consider, for example, the preceding paragraph. The first sentence, *One of the most common writing problems I see in the work of seminar participants is lack of cohesiveness*, establishes the topic of the paragraph. The second sentence defines the term and restates the problem. From there the reader is led smoothly and naturally to the final sentence, which serves as a transition into the next paragraph.

Notice that the third, fourth, and fifth sentences all begin with *writing* and the fourth contains an independent clause that begins with *writing*. This repetition helps to tie the sentences together and in that way contributes to the paragraph's cohesiveness.

I constructed that paragraph carefully to illustrate the principle of cohesiveness. In most writing, however, the cohesive forces are not so easily identified; but they are there. For another example, consider the following excerpt from *The Story of English*, by Robert McCrum, William Cran, and Robert MacNeil. As you read the excerpt notice how the authors lead you gently along by making each sentence relate to the one that precedes it:

> Elizabeth I, the queen to whom so many of these adventures were dedicated, died in 1603. In a surprisingly peaceful transfer of power, James VI of Scotland became James I of England. It was an event of momentous significance. The Elizabethans had initiated a renaissance in spoken and written English. Under the Jacobeans this achievement began to be standardized and disseminated throughout the British Isles, and spread overseas to the New World as the language of a unified nation. James became, at a stroke, the most powerful Protestant king in Europe, and he adopted, for the purposes of foreign policy, the title "Great Brit-

ain." The language of this enlarged state was now poised to achieve international recognition. Of all the ways in which James left his mark on the English language, none was to match the new translations of the Bible ordered in the second year of his reign.

Most good writers make little conscious effort to achieve cohesiveness in their work. Cohesiveness is a product of a good ear and an orderly mind. The student, however, can benefit from paying more attention to the things that make writing hang together and in the process can train his ear and order his mind.

SUBTLETIES OF EMPHASIS AND FLOW

As noted in Chapter 1, writing and speaking are different media of communication. An important difference between them is the methods available for emphasis. Emphasis in speaking comes from gestures, inflection, facial expressions, pauses, and "body language." Emphasis in writing can be achieved through the use of italics, boldface type, underlining, and exclamation points. There are, however, more subtle ways to emphasize.

One of the best ways to emphasize is to use the right word order. Words and ideas that you want to emphasize should come near the end of the sentence. Contrast two versions of the thought expressed in the first sentence of this paragraph.

One of the best ways to emphasize is to use the right word order.

Using the right word order is one of the best ways to emphasize.

The first version makes the point more emphatically than the second by putting the most important idea, *the right word order,* in the latter part of the sentence. Considering the sentence in context, we find that its first part, *One of the best ways to emphasize,* serves as a transition from the previous paragraph. Many writers construct most of their sentences that way. The technique not only puts the emphasis where they want it, but it also facilitates the flow of ideas. Their paragraphs are composed of sentences in which the less important information or the idea at the beginning of each sentence ties in with the more important idea — or anything new that they want to introduce — at the end of the preceding one. Note how the following sentences relate in that way:

There are, however, better ways to emphasize. One of the best is to use the right word order. Using the right word order helps the writer to ensure continuity.

The important idea in the first sentence is *better ways to emphasize.* It flows to *one of the best,* which is the less important idea in the second. New information, *to use the right word order,* is introduced in the latter part of the second. The third sentence continues the process by repeating the old idea, *using the right word order,* at the beginning and introducing the new thought, *to ensure continuity,* at the end.

Rewriting the three sentences to reverse the word order, we get:

Better ways to emphasize are available, however. Using the right word order is one of the best. Continuity is ensured by using the right word order.

The difference between the versions is striking. The first is smooth and natural; the second, choppy and stilted. The first puts the emphasis where it belongs; the second allows each thought to tail off into nothing like the outer ring of ripples on a pond.

The same technique is used to emphasize ideas and information in clauses within a sentence. For example:

Anyone who wants to write well must learn how to use emphasis, and emphasis is more than italics or underlining; of course, such devices are useful, but a skillful writer likes subtler techniques.

In each clause of that sentence, the new or important idea is in the latter part. Compare it with:

Learning to use emphasis is essential to anyone who wants to write well, and italics and underlining are not all there is to emphasis; subtler techniques are favored by skillful writers, even though such devices as italics and underlining are useful.

In long sentences, elements to be emphasized are often placed immediately before punctuation marks. This helps keep long sentences from getting out of control.

Unnecessary repetition, which may be tedious if overused, can sometimes add dramatic emphasis. Example: **The company must invest more in research in order to develop new prod-**

ucts, to compete in the marketplace, and to provide a better return to investors. That sentence could be written, **The company must invest more in research in order to develop new products, compete in the marketplace, and provide a better return to investors,** but the first version has more impact because it emphasizes each of the three reasons for the company's need to invest more in research.

Dramatic emphasis can also be added by departing from the normal (subject, verb, object) word order. For example, **There on the floor in plain sight was the ring of keys I had been searching for.**

An often-overlooked principle of emphasis is the use of understatement, particularly simple, unadorned declarative sentences. The shortest verse in the Bible is "Jesus wept." No adjective or adverb could make it stronger. A point made earlier is worth repeating: If you include too much, you emphasize nothing.

PUNCTUATION AS EMPHASIS

A good speaker uses pauses for emphasis. Pauses are of varying duration, and their length determines their effect on the listener. A good writer uses punctuation marks in much the same way. Different punctuation marks indicate pauses of different "strength," and they have different effects on the reader.

A comma, for example, indicates a short pause and relatively minor emphasis, which accounts for the fact that commas are considered optional more often than are other marks of punctuation. In some sentences the addition of a comma where none is required gives subtle emphasis to a thought. Compare:

> In some sentences the addition of a comma where none is required gives subtle emphasis to a thought.

> In some sentences, the addition of a comma where none is required gives subtle emphasis to a thought.

In the second version, the emphasis on *in some sentences* is slightly greater than in the first.

In conventional usage, a comma before a conjunction is not recommended if a dependent clause follows. For example: **The company began a research program last year and brought**

several new products to market. Some writers would put a comma before *and* in order to show that the new products were the result of the research program and not merely coincidental to it. Whether using the comma in that way can be justified is debatable. It seems to me that using a comma before *and* would make the second clause independent by implying a subject — *it* or *the company*. If emphasis is the goal, a dash is the better choice; thus, **The company began a research program last year — and brought several new products to market.**

TRUST THE EAR

Good writing has a quality variously described as "rhythm," "symmetry," "balance," "cadence," and "style." I call it "ear appeal." What it amounts to is, good writing *sounds* good. True, writing communicates visually; but it also communicates audibly, which is to say the reader "hears" through his mind's ear what he sees on the paper before him. For this reason, the often-advanced argument that the ear is not a good guide to the placement of commas is a specious one.

The lack of ear appeal in writing is easy to discern, but defining the factors that produce it is another matter. Many of the principles discussed in this book — e.g., emphasis, flow, cohesion, word choice, parallelism — relate to how writing sounds. The writer who pays attention to these principles usually produces writing with ear appeal. Conversely, writing that sounds good usually follows the principles of good writing. Beyond that, however, the writer's sense of rhythm will tell him that some words just don't belong together. For example, I wrote in an earlier version of this passage that "the reader's mind's ear hears what he sees on the paper before him." The two possessives together and the juxtaposition of *ear* and *hears* created an unpleasant combination of words. I changed it to "the reader 'hears' through his mind's ear what he sees on the paper before him." The two words work wonders.

Some teachers urge their students to try writing poetry as a way to develop a better sense of rhythm. More practical advice, however, is to read aloud now and then. Try it with samples from articles in *National Geographic* and *Smithsonian* magazine or stories by Ernest Hemingway. Above all, read some of your own writing aloud. You'll be able to tell whether it has ear appeal.

BEYOND TEACHING

It is sometimes hard to tell when teaching stops and preaching starts. At the risk of crossing that line, I want to close this tome by directing your attention to the quotation that appears on the title page of this final chapter.

> Remember that what you write may be your legacy. Give it as much care as you can.

The fact that you have bought this book and have taken the time to read it shows that you're serious about wanting to write better. Whether you aspire to write the proverbial "great American novel" or just clear, functional business communications, the success of your writing will be in proportion to the care you give it. If you diligently apply the principles we have discussed, your legacy will be reader-friendly writing.

Good luck.

Appendices

APPENDIX A

EXERCISE 1

Example Number One: The subject neighborhood, within a 1 mile radius of the property, has an average household income of $44,200 and a medium home value of over $76,000. Within the same radius approximately 72% of the employment base hold managerial, sales, and/or administrative support positions.

This excerpt is reasonably clear, but it is longer than necessary. It did not come from a legal document, but the writer uses pseudo-legal language (e.g. *subject neighborhood*) when plain English is preferable. The writer uses *medium* when he should have used *median*. A shorter version something like this would be better:

> The median value of homes within a one-mile radius of the property is more than $76,000. Income per household averages $44,200. Seventy-two percent of the residents who work are in management, sales, or administration.

Example Number Two: As additional participation interest, the company shall receive the greater of $4,500,000 or 50% of the sales proceeds or net equity value, above the loan balance upon sale of the property to a bona fide third party, at loan maturity, or at refinancing the project. Net equity value represents the total value as determined by sale or appraisal, less the following: 1) actual costs of sale (not to exceed 3%) and 2) the loan balance, excluding any deferred interest.

The writer gets tangled in a tedious explanation of a simple concept. I suggest:

> If the borrower sells or refinances the property, the company will receive, as additional participation interest, $4,500,000 or 50 percent of net equity, whichever is greater. Net equity is the sale price or the loan value, less the costs of selling or refinancing.

Example Number Three: The primary risk associated with this transaction is that the property will be unable to achieve and continue to obtain stabilized proforma occupancy and generate the expected income necessary to support the company's debt service.

The writer of this one is guilty of verbal overkill. *Achieve and continue to obtain, stabilized proforma occupancy,* and *expected income necessary* are phrases that could be eliminated or at least expressed more simply. I would simplify the sentence as follows:

> The primary risk of this transaction is that the property will not generate enough income to service the loan.

Example Number Four: The primary risk in this project is the property's failure to lease-up to breakeven occupancy. The risk is mitigated by the high occupancy in the competing projects of 95%, and the appropriate mix of apartments of 10 studios, the most difficult units to rent with the highest vacancy, to 110 one-bedroom units, to 31 two-bedrooms. This risk is further mitigated by the experience of the borrower team, which includes The Crossing, a highly respected management team specializing in elderly housing facilities primarily in the West.

This excerpt suffers from weak or nonexistent punctuation, and it's windier than a Chicago street corner. And, are "elderly housing facilities" rundown apartments? Note how I have handled the punctuation in my revision. Numbering the mitigating factors help make the writing reader-friendly:

> The primary risk in this project is that the property will not reach break-even occupancy. Mitigating factors are (1) competing projects enjoy 95 percent occupancy, (2) the borrower's respected management team specializes in housing for the elderly, mostly in the west, and (3) the property has a desirable mix of units – 110 3-bedroom units, which are the easiest to rent; 31 2-bedroom units; and only 10 studios, which are the hardest to rent.

EXERCISE 2

In Exercise 2 you were asked to write a business memo based on information provided. Below is the memo the company sent to inform its field force of the change of the name of its Possible Duplicate Coverage Report to Coordination of Benefits Report. It contains 190 words. Compare it with the memo you wrote following instructions in Exercise 2. Is it longer or shorter? Is it well organized? Is it clear, correct, complete, concise, and considerate?

> In keeping with current insurance industry terminology, we are renaming our Possible Duplicate Coverage Report to Coordination of Benefits Report.
>
> A survey of customers in various parts of the U.S. revealed that 97% of them preferred the term Coordination of Benefits over Possible Duplicate Coverage.
>
> With this in mind we have embarked on the process of revising our various forms to reflect this new terminology. On the reverse of this Bulletin is a copy of our most used inquiry, the form 18905. Eventually we will have all other forms, both inquiry and report blanks revised to reflect Coordination of Benefits.
>
> This change in no way affects the way we handle the service, or the way it is billed to the customer. Further, CBBR's and Business Billed Reports will also eventually change.
>
> We believe this change will more appropriately reflect standard terminology that is in use in the industry.
>
> It is appropriate when talking to customers either in sales presentations or handling service requests that we begin to use the term Coordination of Benefits Report.

I would give this memo a passing grade on four of the five C's. It is clear. Except for some missing or misplaced commas, it is correct. Presumably, it is complete, and it is not so badly written as to be called inconsiderate. However, it is far from concise. Here is how it can be shortened simply by striking out unnecessary words:

> In keeping with ~~current~~ insurance industry terminology, we are renaming our Possible Duplicate Coverage Report ~~to~~ Coordination of Benefits Report.
>
> A survey of customers in ~~various parts of~~ the U.S. revealed that 97% ~~of them~~ preferred ~~the term~~ Coordination of Benefits _to_ ~~over~~ Possible Duplicate Coverage.
>
> ~~With this in mind,~~ We have embarked on the process of revising

our ~~various~~ forms to reflect this new terminology. On the reverse of this Bulletin is a copy of ~~our most used inquiry, the~~ form 18905. Eventually we will have all other forms, both inquiry and report blanks, revised ~~to reflect Coordination of Benefits~~.

This change in no way affects the way we handle the service ~~or the way it is billed~~ to the customer. ~~Further, CBBR's and Business Billed Reports will also eventually change.~~

~~We believe this change will more appropriately reflect standard terminology that is in use in the industry.~~

~~It is appropriate~~ When talking to customers, ~~either in sales presentations,~~ or handling service requests ~~that we begin to~~ use ~~the term~~ Coordination of Benefits Report.

The memo can be further shortened and improved by rewriting and reorganizing. My version, which contains 83 words, follows:

We have changed the name of our Possible Duplicate Coverage Report to Coordination of Benefits Report. We are revising all our forms accordingly. On the reverse of this memo is a revised Form 18905.

Only the name has changed. We'll handle the service and bill the customer as usual.

We surveyed some of our customers in the U.S. and found that 97 percent prefer the new name, which reflects industry terminology. Please begin immediately to use Coordination of Benefits when discussing the service.

This version of the memo, besides being less than half as long, is organized to give all the essential facts before offering rationale for the change. I purposely used the new term in the last sentence to reinforce it in the readers' minds.

EXERCISE 3

The sentences in Exercise 3 can be simplified as follows without significantly changing their meaning:

1. The answers are on page 32.

2. A good salesman will make four to six calls daily.

3. Margaret Mitchell was famous for *Gone With the Wind*.

4. We discussed several things at the meeting yesterday.

5. The car is available in red, white, or blue.

6. Here is a list of all medical doctors in and around Philadelphia.

7. There is no shortcut to good writing.

8. This recent book contains a great deal of up-to-date information.

9. We are sorry that you feel you must resign at a time when the club is short of members.

10. The company supported everyone who objected to the new rules.

EXERCISE 4

No amount of editing could make the MediHealth letter good. It is badly written and badly organized. It fails miserably to communicate any coherent message about the company it is supposed to promote. The purpose of this exercise, however, is simply to demonstrate how much writing can be improved by reducing verbal clutter. Compare your edited version with the one below.

Dear _____:

~~One of the more~~ *An* interesting aspect*s* about life ~~here~~ in Savannah in the past few years has been the ~~change of pace associated with its~~ *increase in the number of* health care delivery systems. In the last ~~12 months alone~~ *year*, 5 Health Maintenance Organizations ~~have opened their doors~~ and 3 Preferred Provider Organizations have been established~~.to cite but two developments. One result:~~ ~~E~~mployers ~~such as yourself~~ ~~are~~ today ~~confronted with~~ *have* more options ~~than ever in the ongoing battle~~ to reduce health care ~~benefit~~ costs.

It is ~~with~~in this context that I am writing to ~~update~~ *about* you ~~on~~ MediHealth~~'s progress. In light of our continued growth,~~ I plan ~~to follow up this letter with additional~~ *periodic* updates. ~~about MediHealth.~~

~~Let me begin by reporting that~~ *S*ince January 1 ~~of this year,~~ we have increased our membership ~~by~~ approximately 32 percent, giving us ~~a total of~~ over 3,000 members ~~throughout~~ *in* our 13-county ~~service~~ area.

~~We believe that~~ The ~~single~~ biggest reason for our growth ~~and~~ *is* ~~progress in Savannah has been~~ that, ~~beyond reducing employer~~ *we have reduced* health care costs, ~~MediHealth actually has been able to deliver~~ ~~quality health care~~ without cutting corners. ~~In fact,~~ We continue to get positive feedback from our members about ~~the~~ *our* comprehensive benefits and services. ~~we offer.~~ We ~~take great pride in~~ *are proud* ~~knowing~~ that our commitment to quality health care is recognized. ~~and appreciated by our members.~~

Since its founding 18 months ago, MediHealth has ~~evolved into~~ *become* the nation's largest independent, investor-owned operati~~on~~ *or* of HMOs. Today it operates ___ HMOs in ___ states, ~~which collectively serve an enrollee population in excess of ___~~ *and has more than ___ members.*

Savannah's health care picture will continue to change; ~~rapidly as the balance of the 1980's unfolds.~~ *B*ut MediHealth's perspective is long-term: We seek to serve the community ~~well by contributing to the so-called quality of life here in the most intelligent and consistent manner possible. We envision doing this~~ not only by ~~delivering~~ *providing* quality health care at an affordable cost, but also by broadening our preventive health care. ~~for our members.~~

HMOs are not the sole answer in the ~~ongoing~~ health care "riddle," but ~~HMOs represent~~ *they are* one ~~of several useful~~ alternative*s*. ~~to employers seeking to offer a reasonable array of health benefits to their employees with high quality care and with no financial surprises. Thus, to the extent that you may be re-~~ *If you are* examining your health benefit situation, we would appreciate an opportunity to meet with you to learn first hand what your ~~particular health care~~ concerns and needs are, and then to respond with ~~what we trust will be~~ a thoughtful proposal ~~for your consideration.~~ *meeting them*

~~On behalf of MediHealth, our many thanks for your interest and attention.~~

Sincerely,

John Doe

EXERCISE 5

Expletives and passive-voice constructions are italicized in the sentences below. I have also rewritten each to eliminate the italicized portions. The rewriting has improved most of the sentences.

1. *It* said in the annual report that three new directors *were elected* by the shareholders this year.

   According to the annual report, shareholders elected three new directors this year.

2. *It* is sunny but cold today.

   The day is sunny but cold.

3. *There* was little demand for the product, so it *was removed* from inventory.

   The company removed the product from inventory because it was not much in demand.

4. *There* was cold chicken in the refrigerator. I ate it, and it was delicious.

   I found cold chicken in the refrigerator. I ate it, and it was delicious.

5. *It* is said that the number thirteen is unlucky.

   Some people say the number thirteen is unlucky.

6. *It* is worth noting that *there* are three models available.

   Three models are available.

7. The dog *had been beaten* unmercifully, but it *was treated* by the veterinarian who was there by chance.

   Someone had beaten the dog unmercifully, but a veterinarian who was there by chance treated it.

8. *There* was much fear of espionage during World War II, but *there* was little chance that America *would be invaded* by the Germans.

   Americans feared espionage during World War II, but America stood little chance of a German invasion.

9. *There* is no money in this year's budget for salary increases.

   This year's budget has no money for salary increases.

10. "There you go again," Reagan said.

(This sentence has no expletive or passive voice. *There* is an adverb, not an expletive.)

EXERCISE 6

Using tired words and phrases is the lazy way to write. I suggest you expand the list of overworked words and their alternatives. You probably use many that are common in your business or profession.

in the event that	if
terminate	end
interface	*
early on	early
on a daily basis	daily
at this time	now
close proximity to	near
a check in the amount of	a check for
first established	established
visible to the eye	visible
exact same	same
a week's time	a week
timeframe	period
honest truth	truth
brown in color	brown
relative to	about
thanking you in advance	**
each and every	each
first and foremost	first
one and only	only
refer back to	refer to
in the process of	is
the month of December	December
per your request	as you requested
pursuant to	***
enclosed please find	enclosed is
remuneration	pay
currently	now
forwarded	sent
ascertain	learn
feel free to call	call

thanking you I remain	thank you
utilize	use
interrogate	ask
the undersigned	I, me
expedite	rush, speed
relate	say, tell
communicate	****
above-mentioned	above
at your earliest convenience	*****
for the purpose of	for
optimum	best
due to the fact that	because

Interface is a common and useful verb in the computer industry. In other applications, however, few people agree on its meaning. I suggest not using it except in computer applications. Consider alternatives such as *cooperate* or *work together*.

**Besides being old-fashioned, *thanking you in advance* is vaguely rude. It seems to imply that if the reader does what the writer asks, the writer won't be bothered with thanking the reader, because he will have been thanked in advance. I can't help envisioning a wedding invitation with the notation, "Thank you in advance for your wedding gift."

***I've never been quite sure what *pursuant to* means. Whatever it means, I would pursue a better way to say it.

****Communicate* is a good word, but a more specific word is often a better choice. If you're talking about writing, say *write;* about speaking, say *speak. Communicate* should be reserved for more inclusive uses.

*****Most of the time, giving a specific date gets better results than using the vague *at your earliest convenience*. Something like *I'd like to have your reply by the end of this week* shouldn't offend anyone.

EXERCISE 7

The following passage has been rewritten to eliminate excess words, weak verbs, "dead" sentences, expletives, passive constructions, and tired words and phrases. Notice how much shorter and livelier it has become.

We must first discuss the matter with property owners in the area. Then we'll apply for a construction permit. We will have to consider many factors before deciding whether to proceed. If we must revise our plans, our engineers will develop alternatives to present to property owners. If we encounter too many problems, we can abandon the project.

EXERCISE 8

The grammatical principle violated in each of the examples in Exercise 8 is discussed below. Excepting example number 1, all examples are rewritten to correct the error. Try to apply the principles to your own writing. If you had trouble with this exercise, you need to review the fundamentals of grammar.

1. The president, whose term in office had barely begun when the opposition in Congress, which included members of his own party, capitulated to public opinion, changing the nature of his party leadership.

   I borrowed this example from *The Handbook of Good English* because I could come up with no better one to illustrate a principle of sentence construction. The first thing you notice about the example is that it is impossible to understand. Why?

   President is in the position normally occupied by the subject of a sentence. Anytime you see a subject, your mind tells you to look for its verb. In this instance, the verb that seems to go with *president* is *capitulated.* So far so good: The president capitulated. But wait. You come to *opposition,* which also seems to require a verb to complete a thought. Its position indicates that it is the subject of a clause. Again, your mind tells you to find the verb, but the only available verb is *capitulated,* which is already taken. So, if you assign *capitulated* to *president,* the clause has no verb. If you assign *capitulated* to *opposition,* then the sentence has no verb. The principle is that every sentence and every clause must have a subject and a verb. Write in complete sentences, not fragments. Advertising copy writers love fragments. With a passion. And use them. All the time. Presumably, it gives their writing some kind of special effect. It does. But I won't say what.

   The sentence in the example cannot be rewritten, because its meaning is unknown. No "correct" version is possible.

2. She writes as well or better than many professional writers.

   The correlatives *as well as . . . or better than* cannot be shortened by omitting *as*. The sentence should be **She writes as well as or better than many professional writers.**

3. He either will or already has mailed a check.

   This sentence requires *mail* after *will* in order to be complete. Thus, **He either will mail or already has mailed a check.** Without mail, will is paired syntactically with *mailed*, resulting in the obviously inappropriate *will mailed*. Although words sometimes can be omitted because they are "understood," this is not such a case.

4. Like the manager, the employee's view of the problem was unrealistic.

   This sentence makes an illogical comparison: a manager with a view. The possessive of *manager* is required, making the sentence read, **Like the manager's, the employee's view of the problem was unrealistic.** In that case, *view* after *manager's* is understood. A better way to express the thoughts would be, **The employee's view of the problem, like the manager's, was unrealistic.**

5. He was fired from the job for sloppy work and drinking.

   He might have been a sloppy drinker, but that is not what the writer of the sentence intended to say. As the sentence is written, *sloppy* modifies both *work* and *drinking*. **He was fired from the job for sloppy work and for drinking** is the correct version. Don't omit prepositions that are needed to make the meaning clear. An alternative version of the sentence, is **He was fired from the job for drinking and sloppy work,** does not require repetition of *for*.

6. Billy has either gone fishing with his brother, or his father has taken him to the movies.

   Here we have an example of faulty parallelism (Chapter 4). Good syntax requires that the information on each side of the correlatives *either . . . or* be of the same grammatical form. In this sentence, *Billy has* is not grammatically parallel with *his father has taken him to the movies*, which is an independent clause. The problem is easily corrected by starting the sentence with *either*. **Thus, Either Billy has gone fishing with his brother, or his father has taken him to the movies.** There we have two independent clauses.

7. I like golfing, swimming, and to play chess.

Another example of faulty parallelism, but it's not as subtle as the previous one. Your ear should tell you immediately that **I like golf, swimming, and chess** is the correct version.

8. He is a good employee, but I dislike him taking so long for lunch.

Does the writer of this sentence dislike the employee? Probably not, but that is what the sentence says. What is disliked is the fact that the employee takes too much time for lunch. **He is a good employee, but I dislike his taking too much time for lunch** is the correct version.

9. My dog didn't show up for his supper, and the next day I told my son it was missing.

This sentence provides an example of an unclear antecedent (Chapter 4). *It* could refer to either *supper* or *dog*. We infer from the context that the antecedent of *it* is *dog*, but the possibility of misunderstanding exists. I would correct the sentence by referring to the dog as *he*. Thus, **My dog didn't show up for his supper, and the next day I told my son he was missing.** Referring to a dog as *it* is all right, but switching from *his* to *it* in the same sentence is not.

10. Everyone must do their best to make the project successful.

According to traditional usage, this sentences must read, **Everyone must do his best to make the project successful.** That's because the antecedent of *his*, *everyone*, is singular and therefore cannot be followed by a plural possessive pronoun (*their*). A pronoun and its antecedent must agree in person, number, and gender. In this example, *everyone* is singular in number and gender. By tradition, this requires the masculine for the pronoun. See Chapter 7 and Appendix B for more discussion of this subject.

11. Don't remove the cake from the box if you plan to give it to John.

Here's another example of an unclear antecedent. Does *it* refer to *box* or to *cake?* Rewriting the sentence as **Don't remove the cake from the box if you plan to give the cake to John** eliminates the ambiguity.

12. The resources of the company were significant, but the ability of the owners to make the best use of them was reduced after they became tied up in litigation.

    Unclear antecedents are so common that I have included several examples in order to make you conscious of them. In this sentence, *they* could refer to either *owners* or *resources.* Take your choice. One or the other should be used in place of *they.* **The resources of the company were significant, but the ability of the owners to use them was reduced after the resources** [or owners] **became tied up in litigation.** In many sentences with unclear antecedents, the context allows the reader to make reasonable inferences, and thus serious misunderstandings are avoided. Unclear antecedents often do cause misunderstanding, however, and the conscientious writer will make certain that each pronoun has a clear antecedent even when the context seems to make the meaning unmistakable.

The correct choice is italicized in each of the sentences below. When necessary, an explanation of the grammatical principle follows.

1. The caller asked to speak with (*whoever*/whomever) was in charge of the project.

    This sentence requires *whoever* because *whoever* is the subject of the verb *was.* Confusion arises because of the location of the preposition *with,* which seems to call for *whomever* as its object. The object of *with,* however, is the dependent clause, *whoever was in charge of the project.*

2. The ability to write well, we believe, is one of the many things that (*set*/sets) her apart.

    If you got this one right you deserve a gold star. Most of my students say that the singular subject, *one,* mandates the verb form *sets.* That would be true if *one* were the subject of *sets.* The operative word is *things;* thus, *things . . . set* her apart. If this still gives you trouble, think of it this way: The woman has many attributes that set her apart from other people; the ability to write well is one of them.

3. She did not object to the (employees/*employees'*) smoking in the restroom. In fact, she didn't mind (them/*their*) smoking in the office.

   Possessives are required because it is the employees' smoking, not the employees themselves, that is in question.

4. The company sent (he and I/him and *me*/him and I) to the seminar.

   Him and *me* are direct objects of *sent.* When pronouns appear in pairs, whether subjects or objects, they cause problems for some writers. If this is a problem for you, try reading the sentence with each pronoun separately. Your ear should tell you which ones are correct. No literate person would say **The company sent I to the seminar,** but **The company sent him and I to the seminar** is more common than I like to believe.

5. Address the letter to (whoever/*whomever*) it may concern.

   Whomever is correct here because it is the object of the verb *may concern.*

6. I decided I would go if the boss (*was*/were) going to be there.

   This one is tricky. The notion persists that *if* is always followed by *were.* It's true that *if* often signals the subjunctive mood, which does take *were* as its verb; but *if* indicates subjunctive only for statements that are impossible or untrue, e.g., If I were you . . .; If I were rich . . .. (See Chapter 7.)

7. Her purse, with her checkbook and all her credit cards, (*was*/were) stolen.

   The singular subject, *purse,* takes the verb *was.* The information set off by commas is not part of the subject of the sentence. Remove *with* and the second comma and you have a sentence with a compound subject that requires a plural form of the verb: Her purse, her checkbook, and all her credit cards were stolen.

8. The men or the girl (*was*/were) given the money.

   In this example, *men* or *girl* is a compound subject with two nouns joined by the conjunction *or.* The verb choice depends on which noun is closer to the verb.

9. The men, not the girl, (was/*were*) given the money.

    Men, not *girl,* is the subject. In sentences like this, choose the one that expresses the positive.

10. The committee (*is/are*) qualified to judge the artist's work.

    Both choices are italicized because either could be correct. Usually, *is* would be the better choice. If, however, you wanted to emphasize the qualifications of the individual members, you might select *are.* Collectives such as *committee, group, family,* and *team* appear to be singular, and indeed they usually are; but they can be plural. (See Chapter 7 for more discussion of collectives.)

11. Physics (*is*/are) among the most difficult subjects I have studied.

    Physics is singular and therefore requires *is* as its verb in this sentence.

12. The United States, and most western nations, (*embraces/* embrace) free enterprise.

    United States is the subject. Because *The United States* is considered to be singular, it requires *embraces.* The commas setting off *and most western nations* prevent *nations* from being part of the subject.

13. The United States and most western nations (*embrace*/embraces) free enterprise.

    Here we have the sentence from example 12, but minus the commas. Without commas the sentence has a compound subject, which requires the plural verb form.

14. If I (*were*/was) you, I would write a letter to protest the poor service.

    If I were you obviously is impossible. Therefore, the *if-*clause is subjunctive and *were* is correct.

15. I felt (*bad*/badly) about making the error.

    Badly is an adverb; *bad* is an adjective. The adjective is required here because it describes *I,* not the act of feeling. (See Chapter 8.)

16. "Do not go (*gentle*/gently) into that good night."

    The Welsh poet Dylan Thomas wrote it that way. I would

not presume to question it: **Do not go gentle into that good night/Rage, rage against the dying of the light.**

17. He plays golf much better than (me/*I*).

    If this gives you trouble, think of it as **He plays golf much better than I play golf.**

18. That's (*he*/him) — the man (who/*whom*) you identified at the trial.

    In this sentence, *he* is called a predicate nominative. Pronouns that follow forms of the verb *to be* are in the nominative case rather than the objective. Other examples are found in **This is he, It is I,** etc. In the part of the sentence following the dash, *whom* is the object of *identified.*

19. The data (is/*are*) not yet available.

    Technically, *data* is plural, and you will never be wrong if you use it that way. Nevertheless, *data* is accepted as singular in most uses. See Chapter 8 for more discussion of *data* and other words with irregular plurals.

20. Having coffee and doughnuts in the office each morning (*is*/are) something we all look forward to.

    Having, a gerund, is the subject of the sentence. It requires the singular verb form.

EXERCISE 9

The italicized words in the sentences below are used incorrectly. If you are not certain why they are incorrect, check your dictionary. Some of the words are discussed in Chapter 8.

1. When the police arrived, the body was *laying* on the ground in a *prone* position, staring at the sky with lifeless eyes.

2. The football team was weak on defense, but *it's* offense was *bombastic.*

3. We will *disperse* the funds by January 30.

4. The *heroin* of the story was a teenage model.

5. The basic *criteria* of good writing is *clearity.*

6. The lessee customarily pays the rent in advance, but the *mortgagee* makes his house payment in arrears.

7. Media advertising campaigns and sales promotions are most effective when they are carried out in *tandem.*

8. Six pretty cheerleaders, waving *pom poms, flouted* their youthful exuberance in front of 50,000 fans.

9. Mr. Jones's tie *complimented* his suit.

10. The company's earnings *decreased 200 percent* this year. (Note; this example illustrates not so much an incorrect use of a word as a lack of clear thought. Earnings cannot decrease more than 100 percent.)

11. *Noisome* children are especially *detracting* to older people.

12. This book is *three times as thin* as the other. (Note: A book can be three times as thick, or it can be one-third as thick. It cannot be three times as thin.)

13. The high school *principle* was a man of high *principals,* and he would never sacrifice those principles to add to his principal.

14. In his speech, the President *inferred* that the leak came from someone in the Senate.

15. The shopping center was *comprised of* one department store, a supermarket, and six small shops.

EXERCISE 10

Obviously, the questions following "The Incredible Unflunkable Reading Test" cannot be answered, because it contains little or no specific information about the Pfogbottom clan. Read the version below to get an idea of how the use of the language of control changes your perception of the story.

Senator Pfillmore Pfogbottom has been a U.S. Senator for 20 years. In 1980 he won with 57 percent of the vote. He's not a wealthy man, but before his election to the Senate he earned $250,000 a year. His wife, Pfanny Pfae Pfogbottom, is executive director of the Beltway Voyeur Society and earns $37,000 a year. The Senator is known throughout official Washington as an unparalleled raconteur on the Senate floor and an enthusiastic roue[accent] in his off-duty time. He also plays golf, but he can't make it to his club, Burning Tree Country Club, very often, due to the press of business. With a typical score in the low eighties, he is considered a very good golfer for one who plays only twice a month.

Senator and Mrs. Pfogbottom have two children, Pfineas, who is 17, and Pfyllis, 14. Pfineas plays basketball on his high school team, and the coach describes him as "a scrappy player and a valuable member of the team in spite of the fact that he is only five feet 10 inches tall." Pfyllis loves to read and usually reads four or five books a month. She is, however, addicted to romance novels. Her parents admit she isn't a "brain," but they say she is a B+ student. The only other member of the household is Mrs. Pfogbottom's 70-year-old unmarried aunt.

The Senator is best known for having introduced a bill to prohibit the exportation of microwave ovens to Ethiopia. It was defeated by a margin of two to one.

EXERCISE 11

A situation like this could cause trouble for you and your company. Mrs. Arnold probably is an influential citizen, and people like her are important to you as the company's community relations manager. Besides, her organization is doing important work that is worthy of your company's support. Your task is to inform Mrs. Arnold of the company's decision without losing her respect and friendship. A gracious letter, apologetic but not abject, is required.

The first of the three choices you were given for opening the letter sounds as if it was written by someone whose "parent" was the dominant personality element at the time. (See Chapter 5.) Both sentences are devoted to reminding Mrs. Arnold how much the company has done:

Dear Mrs. Arnold:

Our company has supported your organization for the past several years by allowing you to use our warehouse for your fundraiser. I am sure you will agree that we have gone "above and beyond" the call of duty in exercising our responsibility to the community.

The second choice comes straight from the "child." *Not my decision* and *decided by the "powers that be"* are the typical statements an errant child might make in order to shift to his playmates the blame for his own misbehavior:

Dear Mrs. Arnold:

    I am sorry to be the one to inform you that your organization has been denied the privilege to use our warehouse for this year's fund-raiser. I want you to know that this was not my decision. It is something that was decided by the "powers that be," namely, our legal counsel and our safety director.

The third choice has the preferred adult-to-adult tone. The opening sentence acknowledges the good work Mrs. Arnold's organization does, which should help soften the bad news to come. The second sentence reminds Mrs. Arnold of the company's contribution, but it does so in a way that is not "parent-like":

Dear Mrs. Arnold:

    I recently became manager of community relations for our company, and my predecessor told me about the fine work your organization is doing to support the orphanage. Our company is proud of the small part we have been able to play in that work. For this reason, I'm especially sorry to tell you that we cannot permit the annual fund-raiser to be held in our facility this year.

The next sentence in the letter should begin to explain the reason for the decision. Something like this would be appropriate:

The truth is, Mrs. Arnold, that the event has become *too* successful. Our engineers say that having so many people in the warehouse is not safe. To make matters worse, our insurance company and our legal counsel tell us we may be violating the fire code by using the facility for a large public gathering.

If possible, the letter should also include an offer by the company to do something to help the organization find another place to hold the fund-raiser:

Knowing how much your organization counts on our support and how important this work is to the community, I have asked our plant manager, Bob Smart, to investigate some other possibilities. He will be contacting you promptly so that an alternative arrangement can be made well in advance of the fund-raiser.

EXERCISE 12

The sentences below are punctuated correctly according to generally accepted rules.

1. Margaret Mitchell, author of *Gone With the Wind,* was a native of Georgia; however, she became known throughout the world.

2. The company has offices in Atlanta, Georgia; Tacoma, Washington; Birmingham, Alabama; and San Juan, Puerto Rico.

3. Sally is ten years old; her brother is only three.

4. "The ability to write well," he said, "is one of the most important skills a businessman can have."

5. Before he became president of the company, he was eastern regional manager.

6. Before he became president of the company, he founded another company that manufactured the same products.

7. "Let's eat, Harry; I'm starved," said Bill.

8. What is, is; what will be, will be.

9. The ability to write well, understand complex ideas, think clearly, and speak before a group are attributes that will serve anyone well.

10. "I have nothing to offer but blood, toil, tears, and sweat," said Winston Churchill, the great World War II leader.

11. December 7, 1941, is known as Pearl Harbor Day. President Roosevelt called it "a day that will live in infamy."

12. The United States declared war on Japan in December 1941. The declaration of war followed the Japanese attack on Pearl Harbor.

13. After World War II, the United States led the way to the formation of the North Atlantic Treaty Alliance, known as NATO, which has its objective the defense of Europe.

14. As rich as he is, he still goes out of his way to save a penny or two.

15. The group included first-, second-, and third-grade students.

16. Was it John Kennedy who said, "Ask not what your country can do for you . . ."?

17. Kennedy made that statement, not on the floor of the Senate, but in his inaugural address.

18. In army slang, a "shavetail" is a second lieutenant. The commanding officer is often referred to as "the old man." I was a 22-year-old shavetail and was briefly a company commander. I often wondered whether the men in my company — most of whom were older than I was — called me the old man.

19. The student asked, "Who was it who wrote, 'All the world's a stage, and all the men and women merely players'?"

20. The company has done well in the past two years, but this year is going to be a very difficult one.

APPENDIX B

When "He" Isn't Good Enough
Avoiding a Sexist Pronoun May Also Improve Your Writing
BY VEE NELSON

(Note: The following article originally appeared in *Fulton County Daily Report*, a newspaper for the legal community of Fulton County, Georgia. Although it was directed to attorneys, it contains good advice for all writers. Dr. Nelson conducts business- and legal-writing courses.)

In *State v. Little*, argument arose over the use of *he* in the instructions to the jury. The defendant, a woman, maintained that the trial court made a prejudicial error in the following:

> Under our system of justice when a defendant pleads not guilty he is not required to prove his innocence, he is presumed innocent. The state must prove to you the defendant's guilt beyond a reasonable doubt.

In this instance, the judge overruled the assignment of error, asserting that the sentence puts forth a general principle applicable to all defendants. However, the complaint — and an increasing number like it — raises questions about the prudence of using *he, him* or *his* as the universal pronoun. In business, politics and law, writers are becoming more aware of the problems surrounding the universal *he*, and they are making conscientious efforts to find solutions.

Although the search for solutions received renewed impetus from the feminist movement of the 1970s, people have been looking for alternatives since at least the 19th century. Charles Converse of Pennsylvania, for instance, suggested the word *thon* as a gender-neutral pronoun. The word remained in the dictionaries until the 1950s, though it was apparently little used.

More recently, there have been at least 16 other proposals for a new pronoun. Among them are *tey, co, E, mon, heesh, hir, per* and *na*. Books have been published using *na* and *per*. One university press and the American Management Association have published books using *hir*.

But don't worry. You won't have to write "A defendant has a right to the lawyer *na* wants." The language already has sufficient ways to address the pronoun problem without inventing new words. Here are eight of those ways that allow you to solve the pronoun problem with ease and with stylistic finesse.

1. Change the singular to plural. Often the singular pronoun is not needed, especially when you're referring to a category of people, such as defendants or witnesses. Using the plural creates no ambiguity and eliminates the need for the singular pronoun. There is, for instance, no reason for the singular in this sentence:

> Paragraph 5(c) requires an employer to ensure that his sales representatives comply with the order.

The plural is much better:

> Paragraph 5(c) requires employers to ensure that their sales representatives comply with the order.

Strike the pronoun. Sometimes you don't need a pronoun, so eliminating it can solve both social and stylistic problems. The following sentence needs conciseness:

> The contractor supplies copies of all employee time sheets, and he submits them with complete documentation of all expenses incurred.

2. Striking the pronoun makes the sentence tighter:

> The contractor supplies copies of all employee time sheets and ~~he~~ submits them with complete documentation of all expenses incurred.

The next sentence needs better balance:

> Information provided by a client to a consultant is privileged in the same way as are communications between a lawyer and his client or a physician and his patient.

The balance is achieved by eliminating the pronouns:

> Information provided by a client to a consultant is privileged in the same way as are communications between lawyer and client or physician and patient.

3. Replace the pronoun with an article. A neutral word such as *a, an* or *the* can easily substitute for *he*. The sentence,

> Until the transaction is completed, the seller shall not take any actions that are outside his ordinary course of business,

becomes

> Until the transaction is completed, the seller shall not take any actions that are outside the ordinary course of business.

4. Use the second person instead of the third person. Many times, particularly in giving instructions, writers use the third person (he) when the second person (you) is far more appropriate. Switching to the second person is not only clearer, but it also circumvents any problems with the masculine pronoun. An instruction is implicit in this sentence:

> If the shareholder allows his checks to remain uncashed for six months, his distribution checks will be reinvested into his account at the then-current net asset value.

You makes the sentence far more direct:

> If you allow your checks to remain uncashed for six months, your distribution checks will be reinvested into your account at the then-current net asset value.

Many writers hesitate to use the pronoun *you* because they think it makes the message either too informal or too didactic. Yet, in some contexts, especially instructions, *you* is clearly preferable.

5. Use a noun. Often a noun can easily be substituted for a pronoun. When using this solution, writers usually choose a synonym. For example,

> We want a geologist to be expert witness. We are sure he can supply the evidence we need

can just as well be written:

> We want a geologist to be expert witness. We are sure this specialist can supply the evidence we need.

Sometimes, however, repeating the existing noun produces a desired rhetorical effect. The sentences:

> A respondent must retain records for two years so compliance can be monitored. He must sanction employees who violate the order,

can be rewritten as:

> A respondent must retain records for two years so compliance can be monitored. A respondent must sanction employees who violate the order.

Repeating the noun here is a viable alternative because it emphasizes the person who must act.

6. Rewrite the sentence. Although it may take more time, rewriting the sentence is often the best way to solve the pronoun problem. Shifting words around can eliminate the need for a pronoun. For instance,

> If a plaintiff loses faith in the system, he may never receive compensation for injury

can be rewritten:

> A plaintiff who has lost faith in the system may never receive compensation for injury.

Use *they* for the singular. This suggestion is often frowned upon by those who are firmly fixed in formal grammar. To them, it is totally unacceptable to use the plural *they* to refer to a singular. Although those people are to be admired for holding to the principles of grammar, in this instance they soon may be grasping a grammatical fossil.

In speech, *they* is already widely used as singular, especially when referring to indefinite pronouns such as *each, everybody* and *anyone*:

> Everyone submitted their requests on the first of the month.

> Nobody likes to admit they didn't research the case thoroughly.

Similar use of *they* is also found frequently in writing. Here is an example from *The Wall Street Journal:*

> If another institution takes over the closed bank or thrift, all deposits are to be transferred to the new institution and no one loses any of their principal or interest.

The paragraph sounds natural both in speech and writing. In addition, the expansion of the plural form to encompass the singular has grammatical precedent.

Originally in English there were two forms for the second person pronoun: *thou* as singular, and *ye* as plural. By the 16th century, however, the singular form had disappeared from formal speech, and *ye*, which had become *you*, emerged as the only form for the second person.

We can see the same process occurring with *they*. The plural form probably will not replace the singular entirely; however, it will continue being a supplement. Considering the precedent and the obvious trend, we can safely use *they* in contexts where it sounds natural.

7. Use a compound pronoun. One of the most common solutions, though not the best, is to use *he or she* every time the singular pronoun is needed. This approach works adequately when the pronoun is required only once or twice in a passage.

If, however, the pronoun appears frequently, it is very cumbersome, as it is in the following sentence:

> The agreement requires that the salesperson specifically ask the individual placing the order whether he or she had authority to purchase the products in the dollar amount of the order and requires that he or she specifically state that he or she is authorized to do so.

Although at times *he or she* is appropriate, there are other, more effective, ways to get around the problem. Any of these eight techniques can solve the problems posed by using the masculine pronoun in a universal meaning. One solution that is not advocated here, however, is *he/she* or *she/he*. These constructions are acceptable only in legal contracts and similar formats, in which the inapplicable pronoun will be crossed out. In other contexts, the use of this jury-rigged pronoun is both poor style and poor grammar. There are enough alternatives that produce polished, readable prose without relying on two pronouns tenuously held together with a slash.

As language evolves, the pronoun problem will undoubtedly work itself out. Until that time, however, you have many ways to eliminate sexist implications in your writing. These options are surprisingly easy to exercise, and, as a bonus, they offer variety and strength to your legal writing style.

APPENDIX C

A Checklist for Reader-Friendly Writing

Before you "sign off" on a piece of writing, use this checklist to judge it against the criteria of the Five C's.

Is It Clear?

☐ Is it punctuated for easy reading and understanding? Does your punctuation follow conventional practices?

☐ Have you used words and phrases likely to be familiar to your readers?

☐ Have you used concrete language where precise messages are required?

☐ Is the information organized logically and efficiently?

☐ Is the Fog Index low relative to the kind of material your readers are accustomed to receiving?

Is It Correct?

☐ Have you double checked facts?

☐ Are grammar, spelling, and word use up to standard?

☐ Have you proofread your work carefully?

Is It Complete?

☐ If you received the communication from a colleague, would it tell you everything you needed to know?

☐ Does it answer the questions *who, what, where, when,* and *why?*

Is It Concise?

☐ Is the writing fat-free?

☐ Does it contain only relevant or necessary information?

☐ Have you used relatively short sentences and paragraphs?

☐ Does it contain few passive voice and expletive constructions?

☐ Is it free of overworked words and phrases?

Is It Considerate?

☐ Is the communication necessary?

☐ Is it written to inform rather than impress the reader?

☐ Does it take into account the reader's knowledge of the subject?

☐ Does it establish a common ground with the reader?

☐ Is it free of sexist language or any kind of language that might offend the reader?

☐ Does it have an "adult-to-adult" tone?

☐ Is it clear, correct, complete, and concise?

APPENDIX D

RECOMMENDED

Here is a short list of books that can help you write better:

1. *The Elements of Style,* by William Strunk, Jr. and E. B. White. This book proves the adage that good things often come in small packages. It sells for under $5 in paperback. It's a bargain. Published by Macmillan.

2. *The Writer's Art,* by James J. Kilpatrick. Kilpo has outdone himself in writing this one. Originally published by Andrews, McMeel & Parker, Inc., it's now available in paperback.

3. *How Plain English Works for Business: Twelve Case Studies,* published by the U.S. Department of Commerce and sold in federal book stores. This book contains good examples of how businesses have rewritten complicated documents to put them into plain English. Are you listening, IRS?

4. *Harper Dictionary of Contemporary Usage,* by William and Mary Morris. One of the best usage manuals available. It's especially interesting because it includes comments of the Morrises' usage panel. Published by Harper & Row. My copy is paperback; it's getting dog-eared from use.

5. *Modern Guide to Synonyms and Related Words,* by S.I. Hayakawa. This is an indispensable tool for anyone who wants to use words with precision. It beats Roget's any day. Published by Funk & Wagnalls.

7. *On Writing Well,* by William Zinsser. This former newspaperman writes well when he writes on writing well. I've read this at least half a dozen times. I'll probably read it again. Published by Harper & Row.

8. *Clear Understandings,* by Ronald L. Goldfarb and James C. Raymond. Goldfarb is a lawyer; Raymond is a professor of English. This dynamic duo has produced one of the best books on writing I've ever read. It's subtitled "A Guide to Legal Writing," but the principles it espouses apply to any kind of writing. Random House is the publisher.

APPENDIX E

GRAMMATICAL TERMS

ACTIVE VOICE — The verb form in which the subject is the doer of the action. Example: Ernest Hemingway [subject] *wrote* the novel, *A Farewell to Arms.* (See PASSIVE VOICE.)

ADJECTIVE — An adjective is a word that modifies or describes a noun or a pronoun. An adjective tells which, what kind of, or how many. Examples: *good* food, *red* shoes, *three* aces.

ADVERB — An adverb modifies a verb, an adjective, or another adverb. An adverb tells how many, when, or where. Adverbs often, but not always, end in *-ly*. Examples: go *slowly*, go *fast*, a *remarkably* good book, coming *soon*.

ANTECEDENT — A word or phrase that precedes and defines a pronoun. Examples: I read the *book* and liked it. (*Book* is the antecedent of *it*.) A pronoun must agree with its antecedent in person, number, and gender. Thus, *it* is singular because *book* is singular. (See Chapter 3.)

ARTICLES — *A, an,* and *the* are articles. *A* is used before consonant sounds; *an* is used before vowel sounds. When the letter *h* is not pronounced (as in *honorable*), the correct article is *an*. When *h* is pronounced (as in *historic*), the correct article is *a*. Thus, *an honorable person,* but *a historic occasion.*

CASE — The relationship of a noun or a pronoun to other parts of a sentence. English has three cases: *nominative* (sometimes called *subjective*), *objective,* and *possessive* (sometimes called *genitive*). A noun or pronoun that is the subject of a verb is in the *nominative case.* Examples: *She* is the best person for the job; The *woman* walked into the store. A noun or pronoun that is the object of a verb or a preposition is in the *objective case.* Examples: That is the woman *whom* I saw in the *store.* (*Whom* is the object of the verb *saw; store* is the object of the preposition *in.* The subjective and objective forms of all nouns are identical. The case forms of some pronouns, however, differ. (Examples: *they* v. *them; who* v. *whom.*) Possessives of both nouns and pronouns are formed according to special rules. (See Chapters 6 and 9.)

CLAUSE — A group of words that contains a subject and a verb. By this definition, a sentence is a clause. However, not every clause is a sentence. For example, *whom I saw in the store* has a subject (*I*) and a verb (*saw*), but it is not a sentence. (See DEPENDENT CLAUSE, INDEPENDENT CLAUSE, RESTRICTIVE CLAUSE, and NONRESTRICTIVE CLAUSE.)

COLLECTIVE NOUNS — Nouns that are singular in form but may be either singular or plural in usage. Examples: family, group, couple, number, majority. (See Chapter 5.)

COMPOUND SENTENCE — Two or more independent clauses linked by a conjunction or a semicolon. Example: *Money won't buy happiness, but poverty won't buy anything.*

COMPOUND SUBJECT — Two or more nouns or pronouns joined by *and* or *or* to form the subject of one verb. Example: *John, Mary, Bill, and I were appointed to the committee.* Compound subjects usually require a plural verb. An exception is when the combined nouns or pronouns are considered a unit, as in *The horse and buggy was the main form of transportation in the early 1900s.*

COMPOUND VERB — Two or more verbs that share the same subject. Example: *The car rolled down the hill, jumped a curb, went over the embankment, and came to rest against a large tree.*

CONJUNCTION — A word or words used to join words, clauses, or phrases. Common conjunctions are *and, but, for, or, as, because, yet, therefore, not only . . . but also, unless, either . . . or,* and *neither . . . nor.* Grammarians classify conjunctions according to their different uses, but knowing these classifications is of little value unless you're studying grammar seriously.

DEPENDENT CLAUSES — A clause that does not express a complete thought and therefore cannot stand alone. Example: Here is that article *I clipped from the newspaper.* (See CLAUSE and INDEPENDENT CLAUSE.)

ELLIPSIS — The omission of a word or words that the reader can easily supply for himself. For example, in *To err is human; to forgive, divine,* the reader can easily supply *is* after *forgive.*

Judicious use of ellipses is a good stylistic device in writing; however, words must never be omitted when doing so would cause ambiguity. The term ellipsis is also used to mean the three dots (. . .) used to show omission of parts of quoted material. (See Chapter 9.) A comma is sometimes used to indicated an ellipsis, as in the example above.

GERUND — A verb form used as a noun. Example: *Running* is a popular form of exercise. Gerunds always end in *-ing.*

IDIOM — An idiom is a word or expression that is accepted as correct even though it does not follow usual patterns of construction or usage. For example, *How do you do* is correct English although it cannot be defended in terms of normal construction. It seems likely that use of plural pronouns with singular antecedents will soon be considered idiomatic English — if it isn't already. (See Chapter 7 and Appendix B.)

INDEPENDENT CLAUSE — A clause that expresses a complete thought and thus can stand alone. A sentence is an independent clause. However, independent clauses are usually parts of sentences. For example, *He traveled extensively in Europe, and he earned money by writing for travel magazines* consists of two independent clauses. The clauses could be separated into two sentences. (See CLAUSE and DEPENDENT CLAUSE.)

INFINITIVE — The basic form of a verb, usually preceded by *to.* Examples: *to go, to eat, to explain.* Infinitives function as nouns — subjects or objects. In *To err is human,* the infinitive *to err* is the subject of the verb *is.* In *We decided to eat dinner,* the infinitive *to eat* is the object of the verb *decided.* Note that the infinitive, which is not a verb, nevertheless takes an object — *dinner.* So-called split infinitives — infinitives in which one or more words are placed between *to* and the verb are controversial. (See Chapter 6.)

INTRANSITIVE VERB — A verb that does not take an object. Examples: *run, swim.* A *transitive verb* is a verb that takes an object. Examples: *say, do.* Some verbs can be either transitive or intransitive, depending on how they're used.

NONRESTRICTIVE CLAUSE — A clause that does not restrict, define, or limit the basic meaning of a sentence. A nonrestrictive clause gives additional information, but it can be omitted.

Nonrestrictive clauses are set off by commas. For example, in *My brother, who is an architect, lives in South Carolina,* the nonrestrictive clause, *who is an architect,* is not essential to the meaning; nor does it define *my brother.* Without the commas, *who is an architect* would be a *restrictive* clause. It would imply that I have more than one brother, and it would "define" the one who lives in South Carolina. (See Chapters 3, 6, and 9.)

PARALLELISM — The syntactical device of expressing parallel thoughts in parallel grammatical forms. (See Chapter 3.)

PARTICIPLE — A verb form used as an adjective. Examples: the *running* man, the *flying* airplane. Participles used as adjectives end in *-ing.* Participles are also used to form compound tenses of verbs. In *His knee hurts because he has run too much, has run* is a compound verb in the past perfect tense. *Run* is a past participle.

PASSIVE VOICE — The verb form in which the subject is the receiver of the action. Example: The novel *was written* by Ernest Hemingway. (See ACTIVE VOICE; also Chapter 4.)

PREPOSITION — A word that indicates movement, direction, location, or relationship. Common prepositions include *on, to, about, through, against, from,* and *over.* A preposition must have an object — a noun, a pronoun, a phrase, or a clause. *In the red car* is a prepositional phrase consisting of a preposition *(in),* an object *(car),* and a modifier *(red).* In *Call the office and speak with whoever answers the telephone,* the object of the preposition *with* is the dependent clause, *whoever answers the telephone.*

PRONOUN — A word that takes the place of a noun. Common pronouns include *he, they, we, them, I, me,* and *y'all.*

REDUNDANCY — An unnecessary repetition of meaning. Examples: *hot water heater, active participation, rain shower, consensus of opinion, present time.* (See Chapters 2 and 4.)

RESTRICTIVE CLAUSE — See NONRESTRICTIVE CLAUSE.

SUBORDINATE CLAUSE — A dependent clause. (See CLAUSE.)

SYNTAX — The arrangement of grammatical elements in a sentence to create meaning. (See Chapter 3.)

TRANSITIVE VERB — See INTRANSITIVE VERB.

VERB — A word that expresses action or being. Examples: *run, speak, is, were.*

Index